ADMIRAL HAYWARD,

THANK YOU FOR THE

HONOR TO SERVE IN THE

NAVY YOU BUILT; THE NAVY

THAT SQUIRTS AND HAVE SET

FOR SUCCESS IN THE CONVERSATIONS"

V/R Bill Bk
CAPT, USN

MW00904361

Jihadist Strategic Communication:

As practiced by
Usama bin Laden
and
Ayman al-Zawahiri

William J. Parker III, PhD

Heidi J. Bridges

"Ever since I can recall, I despised and felt hatred towards Americans."
Usama bin Laden interview, 1998 to al-Jazeera Arab Television[1,2]

"We tell America only one thing. What you have suffered until now is
only the initial skirmishes. The real battle has not started yet."
Dr. Ayman al-Zawahiri, Al-Arabiya Television[3,4]

authorHOUSE®

AuthorHouse™
1663 Liberty Drive, Suite 200
Bloomington, IN 47403
www.authorhouse.com
Phone: 1-800-839-8640

First published by AuthorHouse 3/7/2008

ISBN: 978-1-4343-6684-9 (sc)
ISBN: 978-1-4343-6685-6 (hc)

Library of Congress Control Number: 2008900872

Printed in the United States of America
Bloomington, Indiana

This book is printed on acid-free paper.

Contents

Introduction

Whether you consider Usama bin Laden and Ayman al-Zawahiri great Muslim leaders, brilliant strategic thinkers plotting against the West, successful businessmen, professionally-trained scholars, experts in the fields of strategic communication or simply well-organized terrorists, no serious decision-maker or scholar can comfortably argue against the fact that these two men have made a significant mark in the history books. The authors did not write this book to serve as a compendium of our personal opinions; but rather as a resource by which the well-informed may look at many of the significant writings and messages delivered by Usama bin Laden and Ayman al-Zawahiri. Specifically, we looked at how the al-Qaeda leadership uses "strategic communication" to emphasize their points. The concept behind strategic communication will be discussed in detail in Chapter 1. Usama bin Laden and Ayman al-Zawahiri are not pioneers in their efforts to influence the world through word and deed. Many figures throughout history have attempted similar endeavors. Karl Marx and Adolf Hitler were two such people.

Karl Marx's *Communist Manifesto*, Adolf Hitler's *Mein Kampf*, Usama bin Laden's *Fatwas* of 1996 and 1998, and Ayman al-Zawahiri's *Knights under the Prophet's Banner* and *The Bitter Harvest* contain common threads of likeminded individuals with global ambitions. It is important that we develop and apply lessons learned from the Former Soviet Union, Nazi Germany, and al-Qaeda's ongoing efforts of a global jihad. Specifically, World leaders should analyze the aforementioned documents, the leaders who instituted them, the societies who believed in them, and the strategic communication approach taken to accomplish their goals. This book was written in an attempt to provide insight into how to defeat those who threaten World peace in the future.

The *Communist Manifesto*, *Mein Kampf*, the *Fatwas*, *Knights under the Prophet's Banner* and *The Bitter Harvest* are similar declarations of expansionary ambitions. Hindsight demonstrates that these documents are precursors to major warfare. Ideally, when the West initially analyzed each of them, planners would have anticipated their intentions so that aggressive diplomatic efforts and strategic communication programs could have focused on preventing warfare. This certainly does not mean that every time a leader (whether a state or non-state actor) indicates a goal of becoming a superpower that the World is destined for war. However, there are commonalities between the documents discussed here that should be highlighted as indicators and warnings. In the future, these indicators and warnings should trigger governmental actions focused at dissuading conflict.[5]

The **first commonality** among these documents is they are <u>directed at a sympathetic population who felt a sense of oppression</u>. In Czarist Russia, the working proletariat class was incited to revolution by an intellectual Lenin, and his Bolshevik Communist Party who planned and executed the October Revolution (1917). This Revolution was aimed at removing the Czar and attacking the bourgeoisie class. Marx had predicted that such revolutions would 'naturally' spring up as oppressed working class people around the world were depleted by capitalism. Lenin forced the revolution in Russia through his power by an organized communist party and by brute violence. The Soviet Union continued to back its Marxist–Leninist ideology with a massive Soviet military (backed by nuclear, biological, and chemical weapons).

Similar to the situation in Lenin's Russia, many in Nazi Germany actually believed their dire situation was a result of the post-World War I Treaty of Versailles[6], rather than believing they were oppressed by their new government. Hitler was able to use this sensation to his advantage and the march towards an Aryan race began.

In the case of al-Qaeda, Usama bin Laden has used "revisionist history" to argue that U.S. forces are on the Arabian Peninsula to partner with Israel and attack Islam. Usama bin Laden is careful to use a strategic communication strategy, which includes enough kernels of truth to convince some moderate Muslims to believe in his cause and subsequently to believe that Muslims are being oppressed by the West.[7] One could argue that as the size of bin Laden's sympathetic population grows; the Global War on Terrorism will continue to expand as well. Therefore, a successful strategic communication plan, focusing on the hearts and minds of those "fence sitters" who have yet to decide if they want to support a militaristic approach to the future, is crucial in shaping the future.[8]

The **second commonality** among the *Communist Manifesto, Mein Kampf,* the *Fatwas, Knights under the Prophet's Banner* and *The Bitter Harvest* focuses on the leaders themselves. Specifically, <u>charismatic leaders were needed to execute the theory, which was earlier explicated in their watershed publications.</u> Marx, Hitler and bin Laden are <u>gifted communicators</u>.[9] Hitler was a motivational orator and bin Laden uses the internet and media as well as any Prime Minister or President. Lenin (following many of Marx's ideas) incited the Revolution of 1917, which overthrew the Czarist rule. He did it in the name of the 'workers', but Lenin himself was an intellectual. He decided that the Communist Party needed to lead the Proletariat and that they couldn't be left to decide what was best for the State. Usama bin Laden may be the best communicator of this elite group. Because of his aristocratic upbringing and simultaneous willingness to live as a common man, many Muslims respect and listen to Usama bin Laden. Usama bin Laden has reportedly proven his commitment by fighting alongside the mujahadeen during the Afghanistan – Soviet Union war.[10] Usama bin Laden's actions have most likely alienated him from many portions of the Muslim world. This may eventually lead to his downfall. Nevertheless, Usama bin Laden is a charismatic individual who has been able to execute a robust strategic communication plan and ultimately motivate the radical masses to conduct a worldwide jihad.

The **third**, and final, commonality of these documents is <u>they were coupled with a decisive act demonstrating the seriousness of the charismatic leader.</u> Nazi Germany invaded Poland on September 1, 1939 in a demonstration of Hitler's resolve. The decisive act of the Soviet Union was much more subtle. Nevertheless, the continued ruthlessness of Stalin and the ambitious growth of their military combined to demonstrate the decisiveness of the Soviet Union and to remove any doubt that their goal was to become a superpower. Al-Qaeda's decisive act was the first bombing of the World Trade Center on February 26, 1993, followed by the 1998 bombing of U.S. embassies in Tanzania and Nairobi, the attacks of the USS COLE in 2000, and the World Trade Center and the Pentagon in 2001.

These aggressive actions served to send notice to the world that each leader was deadly serious about transitioning the written document into action. An overview of the similarities and differences of Karl Marx,

Adolf Hitler, Usama bin Laden and Ayman al-Zawahiri can be found in Table 1 on the next page. This table provides a "snapshot" of: *The Communist Manifesto, Mein Kampf*, the *1996* and *1998 Fatwas* of Usama bin Laden, *Knights under the Prophet's Banner* and *The Bitter Harvest*. In addition to the documents, the table also provides insight into the life, motivation and decision-making processes of these four famous authors.

Parker-Bridges Analysis of Key Actors, and their Strategic Communication Efforts:

Communist Manifesto
Mein Kampf
1996 and 1998 Fatwas
Knights under the Prophet's Banner and The Bitter Harvest

	Education	Family Pedigree	Key Publications (Year published)	Result of Key Publications	Impact of religion on their actions	Strategic Communication Message	Motivating Principle	Imprisoned for attempted Coup d'etat	Transition from theory to action
Karl Marx	University of Berlin (also studied law); Ph.D. in philosophy from the University of Jena	Well-educated, aristocratic family.	Communist Manifesto (1848)	Basis for the world communist strategy in the 20th century.	Global society will transition in order through the following economic systems: Tribal; Slave Holding; Feudal; Capitalist; Socialist[11]	Class struggle between "The two great hostile camps is destined."[12] – The Bourgeoisie (Propertied Class) and the Proletariat (Working Class)	Socialist Society is superior to Capitalism.	Not imprisoned.	Became a "Revolutionary Communist" in 1843 after moving to Paris, France.[13]
Adolf Hitler	Self-educated. No formal education. Charismatic leader and speaker. (Voracious reader of current events.)[14]	Poor peasant family.	Mein Kampf[15] (Books 1 and 2)[16] (1923)	Lead to the start of WW II in Europe.	Disdain against Catholic Church as a result of not being selected to become a Catholic Priest due to his lack of education.	Aryans were superior to all other humans and should be treated with greater respect due to their race.	Aryan race will rule the world.	Incarcerated for three-years after being convicted of treason following his 1923 "Beer-hall PUTSCH."[17]	1923 "Beer-hall PUTSCH", followed by the invasion of Poland (September 1, 1939).

Usama bin Laden	Attended King Abdul Al-Aziz's University. Degree in Economics (with background in structural engineering and explosives)	Father: Yemen-born. Billionaire and Minister of Public Works following his successes in Saudi Arabia business. Mother: Syrian-born and fourth wife of Mohammed. World traveler and known to wear expensive Western clothes instead of traditional burka.[18]	*Fatwas*: Jihad against Jews and Crusaders; Declaration of War Against Americans Occupying two Holy Places (1996 and 1998)	Clearly defines the enemy as Jews, Americans and Infidels	His interpretation of Islam is the sole driver behind his words and deeds.	The Muslim world will fight to the death or until all "Infidels" leave the Holy Land.	The Holy Land will be ridded of all non-believers.	Not imprisoned, but in April, 1991, he fled Saudi Arabia, after being confined to Jiddah following his opposition to the Saudi-US alliance.	First bombing of World Trade Center (February 26, 1993).
Ayman al-Zawahiri	Medical Doctor; University of Cairo	Egyptian aristocracy	*Knights under the Prophet's Banner* (2001); *The Bitter Harvest* (1991)	Drove jihad in Egypt and later unified al-Qaeda.	Religion and science appear to be the central focus of his actions.	The world is divided into two camps: "The believers" and "The infidels". The most wicked infidels are Jews and Americans.	The nation of Islam will punish "non-believers" and any entity threatening its existence.	Imprisoned from 1981-1984 for ties to the assassination on President Anwar Sadat.[19]	Ties to 1981 assassination of Egyptian President Sadat.

Chapter 1
Strategic Communication:
A Western Perspective

Strategic Communication is more than simply talking on the radio, television, and internet. It exceeds mere articles in the newspaper. Strategic Communication is more than what message we send. It is also how we send a message and who sends it. Deputy Secretary of Defense, Gordon England, in an October 16, 2006 address to the Export Controls Conference in Washington, D.C. made the following comment that Strategic Communication is, "Clearly linking words with actions, and bearing in mind how our actions are likely to be perceived around the world."[20] In a Global War on Terror speech, Secretary England stated, "Strategic Communications is more than just communicating; it is like reading the global information environment like a soldier reads terrain."[21] The Department of Defense is not the only organization using Strategic Communication. As a matter of fact, it is a national-level effort engineered by the Department of State.[22] The Public Affairs organization within the Department of State, under the direction of Ambassador Karen Hughes, describes their role in Strategic Communication as:

1

Effective public outreach requires effective planning. PA's Office of Strategic Communications and Planning provides short- and long-range strategic planning to support the Secretary's effort to bring foreign policy issues to the American people. The office develops strategies to advance the Administration's priority policy issues, shape effective messages explaining U.S. policies in new and ongoing issues and enhance communication with the American people. It coordinates with bureaus throughout the Department, the White House, and other agencies dealing with foreign affairs, and it works with State Department public diplomacy offices to coordinate strategic planning for both domestic and international audiences.[23]

The official definition of "Strategic Communication" as delineated in several Department of State and Department of Defense publications is: "Focused United States Government processes and efforts to understand and engage key audiences to create, strengthen or preserve conditions favorable to advance national interests and objectives through the use of coordinated information, themes, plans, programs and actions integrated with other elements of national power."[24]

While the definition of Strategic Communication is necessary to explicate its requirements, <u>true practitioners simplify Strategic Communication as a compilation of Public Affairs, Support to Public Diplomacy and Information Operations</u>. These three areas formulate the Triad of Strategic Communication as depicted below.

Strategic Communication Triad:

1) <u>Support to Public Diplomacy (SPD).</u> *The National Military Strategic Plan for the War on Terrorism* defines Support to Public Diplomacy as, "Those activities and measures taken to support or facilitate public diplomacy efforts of the Department of State."[25]

2) <u>Public Diplomacy (PD).</u> Joint Publication 3-53, entitled Joint Doctrine for Psychological Operations, defines Public Diplomacy as, "Those overt international public information activities of the USG designed to promote U.S. foreign policy objectives by seeking to understand, inform, and influence foreign audiences and opinion makers, and by broadening the dialogue between American citizens and institutions and their counterparts abroad."[26]

3) <u>Public Affairs (PA).</u> Joint Publication 3-61, entitled *Public Affairs* defines Public Affairs as, "Those public information,

command information, and community relations' activities directed toward both the external and internal publics with interest in the Department of Defense."[27]

4) <u>Information Operations (IO)</u>. Joint Publication 3-13, entitled *Information Operations*, defines *information operations* as, "The integrated employment of the core capabilities of electronic warfare, computer network operations, psychological operations, military deception, and operations security, in concert with specified supporting and related capabilities, to influence, disrupt, corrupt or usurp adversarial human and automated decision making while protecting our own."[28]

Applying Strategic Communication to the Real World

Strategic Communication audiences will change regularly based on the scenario, but in general are divided into the categories of: Friends, Allies, and Adversaries. Chapter 3 of this book demonstrates, in great detail, the efforts made by Usama bin Laden and Ayman al-Zawahiri to address each audience at the right time with the right message. While al-Qaeda does very well addressing the correct audiences, the organization does not have a monopoly on this effort. The West similarly goes to great efforts to win the hearts and minds of the correct audiences in an effort to appropriately shape the environment in a manner conducive to our objectives.

Al-Qaeda has no borders; so the organization, and its members, are often difficult to identify. Still, al-Qaeda is well-funded and fanatical in its approach. For these reasons, the United States, and indeed the free World, is embarked upon a war that will require all instruments of National Power. The instruments of national power—all of which are directly linked to Strategic Communication—are commonly referred to as DIME-FIL (pronounced "DIME FILL"). The letters of DIME-FIL represent the seven primary instruments of national power: Diplomatic, Information, Military, Economic, Financial, Intelligence, and Law Enforcement. Strategic Communication impacts (directly or indirectly) every instrument. So it is incorrect to equate Strategic Communication to only those activities conducted in a public affairs, or media realm.

An example of Strategic Communication follows. If someone points a gun at your head and pulls the hammer back, they are sending you a message. If a nation places 100,000 combat troops off your coast and uses aircraft to drop leaflets telling you to "surrender or die", they are sending a message. Similarly, publishing articles in foreign newspapers contrary to an adversary, changing investment strategies in another country, and offering formal diplomatic demarches are all forms of Strategic Communication strategies. In short, <u>Strategic Communication is actions as much as words</u>.

Now that we have discussed what strategic communication is, we will shift focus to how Strategic Communication could be implemented.

Implementing Strategic Communication

Defining a new concept is relatively easy. Implementing it is much more difficult. Good ideas will continue to originate from academia, think tanks, the private sector and the government. But successful implementation requires intellectual and careful application of all instruments of national power as discussed earlier. Properly implementing a useful Strategic Communication policy requires a consolidated effort across a nation's senior-level agencies, as well as its friends and allies. As an example, if Western Civilization desires to make it clear to Islamic fundamentalists that terrorism will not be tolerated; a cogent and consistent message from a united front of friends and allies must be agreed upon. This is very difficult, since many nations find it difficult to even agree internally. Once the message is agreed upon, the more difficult portion of Strategic Communication – resolution through action – is required. Just like our earlier example of pointing a gun to your head, if the free world were to freeze assets of all nations harboring or supporting terror, the problem may be resolved internal to those nations being starved. This "global market approach" is only one example of how to communicate resolve to a potential enemy. But if the actions are successful, other rogue nations or bad actors may follow suit and stop supporting terror. Conversely, if a nation fails to follow through with threats resulting from terrorist acts, that nation posing the threat loses credibility, and ultimately - power.

Senior communicators (home and abroad) are often used to facilitate Information Operations activities, whereby we send a strong message to a potential bad actor in lieu of formal correspondence. Conversely, good behavior is supported as well. There are times when the best messages a nation can send another country or organization are in the form of money, military aid, or logistical support. As an example, the United States' humanitarian relief efforts following the 2005 earthquakes in Pakistan and the 2004 tsunami in Thailand provided a great opportunity for the World's super power to demonstrate its desire and willingness to do the right thing. This sent many messages to the world - including the fact that the United States was ready and willing to flex its military and logistical might to help others in need. Additionally, the people of the United States were most generous in providing money and support to those in need.

Just as important as the message, the importance of the audience and the venue to address certain audiences cannot be overstated. As an example, senior executives often have better contacts and influence in smaller nations than official government entities. In Africa, for example, many oil and diamond companies have better contacts than the United States Government. This is because they work with the local population and directly impact their daily lives. The civilian businessmen are often trusted to tell the truth (which they should) and are able to communicate directly with the population and government officials. Greater use of non-government organizations like the oil companies is necessary to reach, and properly communicate, a believable message to these audiences.

Similar to who is delivering the message, it is imperative to know how the audience is best contacted. If less than 25% of a particular population watches television regularly, but 98% listen to the radio, a smart communicator will spend money and effort on radio messages instead of television time. The lesson to be learned in these cases is that while themes and messages are important, the delivery vehicle (people, radio, television) is equally important.

Communication Strategies should include an assessment of the information environment. It should outline information objectives, audiences, themes, and actions that support the national leadership's intent. Communication strategies must be coordinated throughout the interagency. Winning "hearts and minds" and influencing other nations and non-state actors cannot be over-emphasized. Spokespersons should reply quickly to queries by focusing on why a specific nation or organization is serious about countering terror and communicate that our nation will support those nations, groups and individuals who join in the fight against terror and tyranny. Public Affairs, Public Diplomacy and Information Operation specialists should look for confirming/supporting public comments and or actions from other nations. Strategic Communication should be aimed at strengthening regional cooperation with the goal being to eliminate terrorism, while at the same time showing a deep commitment to Partner Nation goals.

Strategic Communication can be delivered through Public Diplomacy efforts such as drafting talking points, arranging for public speaking events, responding to media queries, and coordinating press availabilities. It is important to remember that Information Operation efforts include psychological operations. There are various ways to communicate Strategic Communication through Information Operation efforts. Tactical application of loudspeakers, print and media aimed at local civilians or combatants are a few examples of judicious use of Information Operations. The key to take away from this point is that Public Affairs is important, but certainly not the only form of Strategic Communication. There are, however, many ways we can implement Strategic Communication through Public Affairs efforts: brokering press availability for senior leaders (speeches, interviews, etc.), organizing town hall meetings, and writing official press releases are just a few examples.

As written above, the West has worked diligently at constructing and implementing a sound Strategic Communication procedure. Similarly, al-Qaeda's leadership (Usama bin Laden and Ayman al-Zawahiri in particular) carefully implements its own Strategic Communication plans. Chapter 3 clearly demonstrates the efforts Usama bin Laden and Ayman al-Zawahiri go to in order to deliver the right message to the right audience at the right time. As an example, certain audiences are re-visited annually by the two principle al-Qaeda authors. These audiences include: the United States government, the United States population; the Muslim world; friends and allies of the West (particularly the United States); and nations and organizations considered "fence sitters" (which have not decided if they will support al-Qaeda or the West).

The United States and many other countries have recently joined forces to establish a strategic approach for delineating well-vetted and consistent themes and messages to our friends, allies, and adversaries.

This concept of Strategic Communication is the result of considerable work by the United States' Departments of State and Defense, as well as many other agencies and nations. While the definition of Strategic Communication is firmly defined, the combination of Public Affairs, Support to Public Diplomacy and Information Operations are the three tiers of Strategic Communication by which all efforts are focused. Significant additional emphasis is being placed on the non-public affairs efforts, since very often actions speak louder than words. Examples include freezing and seizing assets of those who support, train and harbor terrorists in addition to speaking with one voice across all sectors of the national government. Strategic Communication is considered "winning the hearts and minds" of other nations and organizations. This can only be accomplished through a comprehensive and focused plan. The United States, and our friends and allies, are moving in the right direction to accomplish the task of freedom with minimal loss of property or life.

America, like much of the World, is a just and fair nation and will continue to apply the moral and legal rules of warfare, while systematically reducing the terrorists' scourge from this earth. Understanding the threat (and potential threat) and applying a solid Strategic Communication plan aimed at winning the hearts and minds of those "fence sitters" and those who would otherwise do us harm is a key instrument of our success as a nation and World.

Chapter 2
Principle Jihadist Actors

"We are not faced with a social problem, which liberal policies and public money can solve; we are facing dedicated murderers. If we are to craft serious and effective policies to combat them, we must begin by recognizing the uncompromising depths of their hatred."

Kenneth Timmerman, *Preacher's of Hate*

Before delving into a detailed discussion of the writings, principles and policies of Usama bin Laden and Ayman al-Zawahiri, it is important to provide a brief background on these two world figures.

Usama bin Laden[29]

Usama bin Laden (also known as Usama Bin Muhammad Bin Ladin, Shaykh Usama Bin Ladin, the Prince, the Emir, Abu Abdallah, Mujahid Shaykh, Hajj, the Director)[30] was born in Riyadh, Saudi Arabia on July 30, 1957. Usama bin Laden was the seventeenth of 52 children. He is the last son of the powerful Muhammed Bin Laden. His Syrian mother, according to Maryanne Weaver of The New Yorker, was not only beautiful, but well beyond her times for a Muslim woman.[31] Usama bin Laden spent his youthful summers with his mother in Syria through age 17. While this woman had significant influence on Usama bin Laden's Syrian contacts and views of the West, his father remains his primary influence. His father, Muhammed Bin Laden, grew up in the northern section of Yemen and migrated to Saudi Arabia in 1927. By 1931 he had started the Saudi Bin Laden group, which continues to be one of the most influential and financially successful corporations in Saudi Arabia today. Usama bin Laden not only gained from his fathers engineering and business prowess, but continues to take advantage of the elder's vast contacts in Yemen and within the Saudi family. Muhammed Bin Laden obtained his vast fortune, which many estimate to be in excess of 5 billion dollars, by originally building well-constructed palaces for the Saudi royal family at a financial loss to his company. By many accounts, this endeared Muhammed Bin Laden to the Saudi royal family; particularly Abdul al-Aziz and his brother, King Faisal. Muhammed so impressed King Faisal that he was appointed as the King's Minster of Public Works. Muhammed Bin Laden died suddenly when his plane crashed in 1968. His eldest son, Salem continued the family business and close ties with the Royal family until his untimely death in 1988. Salem, like his father, also died in a plane crash. In the book, "*Through our Enemies' Eyes*", Usama bin Laden in a 1997 interview with Hamid Mir, is quoted as saying, "I worked on the expansion of the Al-Aqasa Mosque. During the early years of my life, I received training in the use of explosives for construction work and demolition of mountains."[32]

Usama bin Laden's education remains somewhat of a mystery. Clearly he attended King Abdul Al-Aziz's University. There is debate over whether he actually graduated and whether his course of study focused on engineering or economics.[33] What is clear about Usama bin Laden's time at the University is that he studied the earliest Muslim scholars. Some time between his late teenage years and early years at King Abdul Al-Aziz's University, he transformed himself into an exceptionally pious and fundamental Muslim. According to Christiane Amanpour of CNN's report entitled, "In the Footsteps of Bin Laden", Usama bin Laden appeared to be a better follower, than leader, in his earlier teenage years. He enjoyed watching Bruce Lee and John Wayne movies; was an avid soccer player, and began to focus on his Muslim religious beliefs - consistently attending Mosque five times daily. His piety increased as he moved through his later teenage years and early adulthood, living in less-than-optimal housing conditions and taking long excursions into the desert with the bare minimum of supplies.[34]

By age 22, Usama bin Laden was playing a critical role in developing Maktabu l-khidamat (MAK. Also called, The Afghan Services Bureau). According to Bruce Lawrence, in his book entitled *Messages To The World: The Statements Of Osama Bin Laden*, MAK "Played a major role during the Soviet-Afghanistan war, training an estimated 10,000 *mujahidin* and dispersing around $2 billion in donations sourced through a network of offices around the world, including the USA. With the wars end, there seems to have been a difference in opinion between Azzam and bin Laden over the future direction of MAK. Azzam wanted to use the network and its resources to help install an Islamic state in postwar Afghanistan; bin-Laden - influenced by the Egyptian members of the Muslim Brotherhood, including Ayman al-Zawahiri and Omar Abdel Rahman – wanted to use it to fund a global *jihad*. When Azzam and his sons was [were] killed by a land mind in Peshawar on November 24 1989, bin Laden assumed control of MAK."[35]

In concert with Palestinian Muslim Brotherhood leader, Abdallah Azzam, bin Laden recruited and trained over 10,000 Arabs to serve as troops in the fight against the vastly superior Soviet Union. Many of the survivors of this war would go on to lead Al-Qa'ida (the Base), which was founded by Osama bin Laden in 1988. The tie between the Central Intelligence Agency and Makhtab al-Khidamat continues to be a point of debate. According to Tore Kjeilen, Editor of "Encyclopedia of the Orient" the Central Intelligence Agency has never denied MAK received funding or training by the CIA.[36] Conversely, Richard Miniter in his book, *Disinformation*, quotes Abdullah Anas in a September 12, 2004 French television program entitled "Zone Interdit" as saying, "If you say there was a relationship in the sense that the CIA used to meet with Arabs, discuss with them, prepare plans with them, and to fight with them – it never happened."[37] Miniter's book also quotes the author of *Taliban*, Ahmed Rashid as stating, "...funding for bin Laden's organization came from "Saudi Intelligence, the Saudi Red Crescent, the World Muslim League and private donations from Saudi princes and mosques."[38] Finally, Richard Miniter quotes CNN's Peter Bergen[39] in what is possibly the most accurate assessment of the relationship between the CIA and Usama bin Laden, when he states, "While the charges that the CIA was responsible for the rise of the Afghan Arabs might make good copy, they don't make good history. The truth is more complicated, tinged with varying shades of gray. The United States wanted to be able to deny that the CIA was funding the Afghan war, so its support was funneled through Pakistan's Inter-Services Intelligence Agency (ISI). ISI in turn made the decisions about which Afghan factions to arm and train, tending to favor the most Islamist and pro-Pakistan. The Afghan Arabs generally fought alongside those factions, which is how the charge arose that they were creatures of the CIA. There was simply no point in the CIA and Afghan Arabs being in contact with each other. The Afghan Arabs functioned independently and had their own sources of funding. The CIA did not need the Afghan Arabs, and the Afghan Arabs did not need the CIA. So the notion that the Agency funded and trained the Afghan Arabs is, at best, misleading. The "let's blame everything bad that happens on the CIA" school of thought. vastly overestimates the Agency's powers both for good and ill."[40]   The Department of State, on its website[41] entitled, USINFO.STATE.GOV, has offered an official statement that, "...Numerous comments in the media recently have reiterated a widely circulated **but incorrect** notion that the CIA once had a relationship with Usama bin Laden. For the record, you should know that the CIA never employed, paid, or maintained any relationship whatsoever with Bin Laden (emphasis in original).

In summary:

+ U.S. covert aid went to the Afghans, not to the "Afghan Arabs."
+ The "Afghan Arabs" were funded by Arab sources, not by the United States.
+ United States never had "any relationship whatsoever" with Osama bin Laden.
+ The Soviet invasion of Afghanistan, Arab backing for the "Afghan Arabs," and bin Laden's own decisions "created" Osama bin Laden and al Qaeda, not the United States."[42]

Al-Qaeda is described by the National Counterterrorism Center as, "Established by Usama Bin Ladin in 1988 with Arabs who fought in Afghanistan against the Soviet Union. Al-Qa'ida's goal is uniting Muslims to fight the West, especially the United States, as a means of defeating Israel, overthrowing regimes al-Qa'ida deems "non-Islamic," and expelling Westerners and non-Muslims from Muslim countries. Al-Qa'ida's eventual goal is the establishment of a pan-Islamic caliphate throughout the world. Al-Qa'ida issued a statement in February 1998 under the banner of "the World Islamic Front for Jihad Against the Jews and Crusaders," saying it was the duty of all Muslims to kill US citizens – civilian and military – and their allies everywhere. The group merged with the Egyptian Islamic Jihad (al-Jihad) in June 2001, renaming itself "Qa'idat al-Jihad." On 11 September 2001, 19 al-Qa'ida suicide attackers hijacked and crashed four US commercial jets – two into the World Trade Center in New York City, one into the Pentagon near Washington, D.C., and a fourth into a field in Shanksville, Pennsylvania – leaving nearly 3,000 people dead or missing. Al-Qa'ida also directed the 12 October 2000 attack on the USS Cole in the port of Aden, Yemen, killing 17 US sailors and injuring another 39, and conducted the bombing in August 1998 of the US Embassies in Nairobi, Kenya, and Dar es Salaam, Tanzania, that killed at least 301 people and injured more than 5,000 others. From 2002 to 2005, al-Qa'ida, using its own operatives or surrogates and sympathetic groups, backed attacks in Tunisia, Indonesia, Kenya, Turkey, Saudi Arabia, and other countries. In 2005 bin Ladin's deputy, Ayman al-Zawahiri, publicly claimed unspecified al-Qa'ida involvement in the 7 July 2005 bombings in the United Kingdom, although investigation of responsibility continues.

In October 2004, Abu Mus'ab al-Zarqawi pledged allegiance to Usama bin Ladin and as a result of the merger changed his group's name to al-Qa'ida in Iraq (Tanzim Qa'idat al-Jihad fi Bilad al-Rafidayn). Al-Qa'ida in Iraq has become the premier jihadist group in the region, focusing on Iraq and the Levant."[43]

According to the MIPT Terrorism Knowledge Base website, "Zarqawi's letter to Bin Laden revealed many problems that the former believed al-Qaeda in the Land of the Two Rivers would face in the coming years. The Sunni insurgent leader pointed out that as American forces are drawn down or removed from the front lines and indigenous Iraqi forces take their place, attacks perpetrated against security forces will increasingly be seen as anti-Iraqi attacks, rather than anti-occupation ones. Zarqawi confessed that his fighters' freedom of movement has become increasingly restricted and that the "future has become frightening". The local Sunni Iraqi resistance is inexperienced and has been unwilling to sacrifice for the cause, whereas battle-tested foreign mujahedin are too small in number to affect significant change. Zarqawi went on to complain that the Sunni Iraqi masses have "no firm principles" and that "their religion is mercurial.".…"[44]

Dr. Ayman al-Zawahiri[45]

Dr. Ayman al-Zawahiri (also known as Abu Muhammad, Abu Fatima, Muhammad Ibrahim, Abu Abdullah, Abu al-Mu'iz, The Doctor, The Teacher, Nur, Ustaz, Abu Mohammed, Abu Mohammed Nur al-Deen, Abdel Muaz, Dr. Ayman al-Zawahiri)[46] was born June 19, 1951[47] in

Cairo, Egypt.[48] He is the author of numerous articles, memos and other publications to include: *The Bitter Harvest* and *Knights under the Prophet's Banner*. He is believed to be the "true brains" and "master planner" in Usama bin Laden's Al-Qaeda. Dr. Ayman al-Zawahiri graduated magna cum laude in 1974 with a Medical Degree from Cairo University. Four years later, he received a Masters Degree in surgery. One year later, in 1979 he married Izzat Ahmad Nuwair. His wife held a degree from Cairo University in Philosophy. Details of Ayman al-Zawahiri's immediate family have been purposefully difficult to obtain. It is believed, however, that his first daughter was born in Cairo; additionally he and his wife Izzat have had one son and three daughters in other regions of the world.[49] It is reasonable to assume that Ayman al-Zawahiri was significantly influenced by the book, *Ma'alim Ala Al-Tariq*. This piece interpreted as "sign posts on the road" looks at the world in a binary fashion. Specifically, this 1957 work assumes that the world is separated into two categories – the first being infidels and the second, believers. In reading Ayman al-Zawahiri's works to include *Knights under the Prophet's Banner*, it is clear that he equates believers to those who follow Shari'a Law. If the binary assessment of our world, as Ayman al-Zawahiri interprets it, is assumed true, then it is assumed that the infidels are guided by a less-than-pure set of laws. Additionally, in his 1991 work, entitled *The Bitter Harvest*, Ayman al-Zawahiri clearly articulates his belief that "true Muslims" will see "democracy" as the enemy that must be destroyed, since only Allah (through his people) should be placed in a position requiring allegiance. In other words, Zawahiri believes that allegiance to any entity other than Allah is strictly forbidden.

Ayman al-Zawahiri became an active member of The Association of the Followers of Muhammad's Path at age 15. This organization is considered an Islamic Fundamentalist support group. One year later, at age 16, Ayman al-Zawahiri became an active member of the Jihadist movement within The Association of the Followers of Muhammad's Path. By 1974, it is predicted that he was trained in the use of explosives and weapons. At the early age of 15, Ayman al-Zawahiri had already developed a plot aimed at overthrowing the Egyptian Government. This focus continued and in 1981 he was imprisoned, for what would later be only three-years as a result of dealing weapons, after Anwar Sadat's assassination. By 1985 Ayman al-Zawahiri had fled Egypt for safe haven in Saudi Arabia. He migrated to Peshawar with the ambition of improving al-Jihad in company with Dr. Fadl. Although Ayman al-Zawahiri was part of a successful military campaign against the Soviet occupied Afghanistan, his attempt to wage war (from Sudan) against Egypt was a total disaster for his organization. By 1996 Ayman al-Zawahiri and Usama bin Laden combined forces between al-Qaeda and al-Jihad. As offered by the Pulitzer Prize winning author Lawrence Wright in his book, *The Looming Tower, Al-Qaeda and the Road to 9/11*, Ayman al-Zawahiri understood that if this new union was to succeed they must learn past history where radical Islamist groups lacked a precise plan and organizational continuity. Specifically, Mr. Wright states, "In January 1998, Zawahiri began writing a draft of a formal declaration that would unite all of the different mujahideen groups that had gathered in Afghanistan under a single banner. It would turn the movement away from regional conflicts and toward a global Islamic jihad against America. The language was measured and concise, in comparison with bin Laden's declaration of war two years before. Zawahiri cited three grievances against the Americans. First, the continuing presence of American troops in Saudi Arabia seven years after the end of the Gulf War. "If some people have formally debated the fact of the occupation, all the people of the peninsula have now acknowledged it," he observed. Second, America's intention to destroy Iraq, as evidenced by the death of what he said was more than a million civilians. Third, the American goal of propping up Israel by incapacitating the Arab states, whose weakness and disunion are Israel's only guarantee of survival."[50] These three "grievances" were the basis behind the February 23, 1998 Fatwa, commonly referred to as "Jihad Against Jews and Crusaders". This watershed document was signed by Shaykh Usamah Bin-Muhammad Bin-Ladin; Ayman al-Zawahiri, amir of the Jihad Group in Egypt; Abu-Yasir Rifa'i Ahmad Taha, Egyptian Islamic Group; Shaykh Mir Hamzah, secretary of the Jamiat-ul-Ulema-e-Pakistan; Fazlur Rahman, amir of the Jihad Movement in Bangladesh.[51]

Ayman al-Zawahiri is on the FBI's Most Wanted Terrorist List and has been indicted for the 1998 bombings of two US Embassies in Africa. Of interest, beginning in 2003, Dr. Ayman al-Zawahiri has been regularly seen as the principle spokesman for al-Qaeda. Additionally, Ayman al-Zawahiri and Usama bin Laden are more regularly addressed as the "co-leaders" of al-Qaeda. This is a fundamental shift from the earlier organizational construct which had regularly placed Ayman al-Zawahiri as the # 2 man in al-Qaeda.

The table on the next page provides a summary of important facts about Usama bin Laden and Ayman al-Zawahiri in a side-by-side comparative format.

Usama bin Laden and Ayman al-Zawahiri Fact Sheet

	Usama bin Laden	Ayman al-Zawahiri
Date of Birth	July 30, 1957[52]	June 19, 1951
Place of Birth	Saudi Arabia	Egypt
Citizenship	Saudi Arabia	Egypt
Language	Arabic/Pashtu	Arabic/French
Bloodline of Parents	Yemen (father) Syria (mother)	Egyptian
Socio-Economic Status	Father: Billionaire and Minister of Public Works	Parents: Aristocratic
Personal Wealth	About 250 Million	Believed to be insignificant.[53]
Education	Attended King Abdul Al-Aziz's University. Degree in Economics (or Engineering)	Medical Doctor University of Cairo
Religion	Muslim	Muslim
Professional Training	Business Entrepreneur	Surgeon
Organizations Founded	MAK co-founded with Asad. Al-Qaeda Note: Bin Laden and Zawahiri decided that the Egyptian Islamic Jihad would focus on Egypt and al-Qaeda would focus on multi-national and global issues.	Egyptian Islamic Jihad. Note: Bin Laden and Zawahiri decided that the Egyptian Islamic Jihad would focus on Egypt and al-Qaeda would focus on multi-national and global issues.
Marital Status/Family	First wife: Najwah Ghanem (his first cousin, m. 1974)	Wife and four children reported to have been killed in December, 2001 as a result of combat operations.[54] Two daughters may still be alive.
Legal Charges/Convictions	Isolated to Jiddah, Saudi Arabia in 1989. "Usama Bin Laden is wanted in connection with the August 7, 1998, bombings of the United States Embassies in Dar es Salaam, Tanzania, and Nairobi, Kenya. These attacks killed over 200 people. In addition, Bin Laden is a suspect in other terrorist attacks throughout the world."[55]	Charged and imprisoned for being connected to the assassination of Anwar Sadat
Books/Major Documents	*Fatwas*: Jihad against Jews and Crusaders; Declaration of War Against Americans Occupying two Holy Places (1996 and 1998)	*Knights under the Prophet's Banner*; *The Bitter Harvest*
Countries Fled To	Afghanistan, Sudan and Pakistan[56]	Saudi Arabia and Afghanistan (fled a year after prison release)

Chapter 3
Strategic Communication: A Jihadist Approach

**(Words and deeds by Usama bin Laden
and Ayman al-Zawahiri)**

This section provides the reader with detailed examples of the strategic communication methodology used by Usama bin Laden and Ayman al-Zawahiri. Because the *Fatwas* of 1996 and 1998 are so strategically significant, we offer these, in their entirety and at the beginning of this chapter. Following the analysis of these two *Fatwas*, the chapter continues with a chronological representation of key Jihadist themes and messages. These themes and messages represent the words and deeds of the senior al-Qaeda leadership. Before discussing Usama bin Laden's 1996 and 1998 *Fatwas*, a brief discussion of *Fatwas* and Jihads is warranted.

Fatwas

First and foremost, it is critical to understand who can issue a Fatwa. According to Sohail H. Hashami, author of *Islamic Political Ethics*, a

Fatwa is a "nonbinding legal opinion rendered by religious scholars, the *mufti*."[57] The Islamic website, www.IslamTomorrow.com further defines a Mufti as "an attorney, who in Islamic law writes his opinion (fatwa or futwa) on legal subjects for private clients or to assist judges…only in the fields of marriage, divorce and inheritance are the *Fatwas* legally binding…"[58] Regardless of whether a fatwa could apply to a public issue, it is not legally binding and cannot be issued, according to Islamic law, by Usama bin Laden. Because U.S. troops are occupying regions (including Iraq, Saudi Arabia and Afghanistan) his fatwa could suggest some validity if the Qur'an is accepted as an authoritative and acceptable moral publication by everyone in the region.

Two Forms of Jihad

Jihad can be interpreted as a "Struggle" or "Effort" within the heart and soul of an individual Muslim or a peaceful attempt to conform non-believers in the ways of Islam.[59] Jihad can also be interpreted as a "holy war". This second form of Jihad, is found in the later portions of the Qur'an (22:39-40) and at first glance appears to transition Muhammad from a non-violent prophet to holy warrior in the name of God.[60] Specifically, and depending on which Muslim scholar is studied, this section of the Qur'an possibly shows God allowing military action for the purposes of defending Muslims and expanding the territory of Islam. If the Qur'an is read chronologically, God (Allah) tells Muhammad, through the Archangel Gabriel, that Jihad is an internal struggle within the heart of the Muslim and is only used in its militaristic sense to extend the boundaries of Islam or defend its religion.[61]

The Muslim scholar, Bassam Tibi, offers the following morally and logically flawed statement when discussing Jihad and the West:

"The Western distinction between just and unjust wars linked to specific grounds for war is unknown in Islam. Any war against unbelievers, whatever its immediate ground, is morally justified. Only in this sense can one distinguish just and unjust wars in the Islamic tradition. When Muslims wage war...for the dissemination of Islam, it is a Just War...When non-Muslims attack Muslims, it is an unjust war. The usual Western interpretation of jihad as a "Just War" in the Western sense is, therefore, a misreading of the Islamic concept."[62]

Usama bin Laden first formalized his ideology and vision in 1996 by issuing his first fatwa, which has been described as a "Declaration of War". This declaration is actually a summary of the 1991 *Letter of Protest* and the 1992 *Memorandum of Advice*. In this document, Usama bin Laden declares a "defensive jihad" against the Americans for their occupation of the Kingdom of Saudi Arabia. Usama bin Laden's strategic message focuses on expelling the American occupiers from the land of Muhammad.

August 1996. "Declaration of War against the Americans Occupying the Land of the Two Holy Places"[63]

"Praise be to Allah, we seek His help and ask for his pardon. We take refuge in Allah from our wrongs and bad deeds. Who ever been guided by Allah will not be misled, and who ever has been misled, he will never be guided. I bear witness that there is no God except Allah-no associates with Him- and I bear witness that Muhammad is His slave and messenger.

{O you who believe! be careful of -your duty to- Allah with the proper care which is due to Him, and do not die unless you are Muslim} (Imraan; 3:102), {O people be careful of -your duty to- your Lord, Who created you from a single being and created its mate of the same -kind- and spread from these two, many men and women; and be careful of -your duty to- Allah , by whom you demand one of another -your rights-, and (be careful) to the ties of kinship; surely Allah ever watches over you} (An-Nisa; 4:1), {O you who believe! be careful- of your duty- to Allah and speak the right word; He will put your deeds into a right state for you, and forgive you your faults; and who ever obeys Allah and his Apostle, he indeed achieve a mighty success} (Al-Ahzab; 33:70-71).

Praise be to Allah, reporting the saying of the prophet Shu'aib: {I desire nothing but reform so far as I am able, and with non but Allah is the direction of my affair to the right and successful path; on him do I rely and to him do I turn} (Hud; 11:88).

Praise be to Allah, saying: {You are the best of the nations raised up for -the benefit of- men; you enjoin what is right and forbid the wrong and believe in Allah} (Aal-Imraan; 3:110). Allah's blessing and salutations on His slave and messenger who said: (The people are close to an all encompassing punishment from Allah if they see the oppressor and fail to restrain him.)

It should not be hidden from you that the people of Islam had suffered from aggression, iniquity and injustice imposed on them by the Zionist-Crusaders alliance and their collaborators; to the extent that the Muslims blood became the cheapest and their wealth as loot in the hands of the enemies. Their blood was spilled in Palestine and Iraq. The horrifying pictures of the massacre of Qana, in Lebanon are still fresh in our memory. Massacres in Tajakestan, Burma, Cashmere, Assam, Philippine, Fatani, Ogadin, Somalia, Erithria, Chechnia and in Bosnia-Herzegovina took place, massacres that send shivers in the body and shake the conscience. All of this and the world watch and hear, and not only didn't respond to these atrocities, but also with a clear conspiracy between the USA and its' allies and under the cover of the iniquitous United Nations, the dispossessed people were even prevented from obtaining arms to defend themselves.

The people of Islam awakened and realised that they are the main target for the aggression of the Zionist-Crusaders alliance. All false claims and propaganda about "Human Rights" were hammered down and exposed by the massacres that took place against the Muslims in every part of the world.

The latest and the greatest of these aggressions, incurred by the Muslims since the death of the Prophet (ALLAH'S BLESSING AND SALUTATIONS ON HIM) is the occupation of the land of the two Holy Places -the foundation of the house of Islam, the place of the revelation, the source of the message and the place of the noble Ka'ba, the Qiblah of all Muslims- by the armies of the American Crusaders and their allies. (We bemoan this and can only say: "No power and power acquiring except through Allah").

Under the present circumstances, and under the banner of the blessed awakening which is sweeping the world in general and the Islamic world in particular, I meet with you today. And after a long absence, imposed on the scholars (Ulama) and callers (Da'ees) of Islam by the iniquitous crusaders movement under the leadership of the USA; who fears that they, the scholars and callers of Islam, will instigate the Ummah of Islam against its' enemies as their ancestor scholars-may Allah be pleased with them- like Ibn Taymiyyah and Al'iz Ibn Abdes-Salaam did. And therefore the Zionist-Crusader alliance resorted to killing and arresting the truthful Ulama and the working Da'ees (We are not praising or sanctifying them; Allah sanctify whom He pleased). They killed the Mujahid Sheikh Abdullah Azzaam, and they arrested the Mujahid

Sheikh Ahmad Yaseen and the Mujahid Sheikh Omar Abdur Rahman (in America).

By orders from the USA they also arrested a large number of scholars, Da'ees and young people - in the land of the two Holy Places- among them the prominent Sheikh Salman Al-Oud'a and Sheikh Safar Al-Hawali and their brothers; (We bemoan this and can only say: "No power and power acquiring except through Allah"). We, myself and my group, have suffered some of this injustice ourselves; we have been prevented from addressing the Muslims. We have been pursued in Pakistan, Sudan and Afghanistan, hence this long absence on my part. But by the Grace of Allah, a safe base is now available in the high Hindukush mountains in Khurasan ; where--by the Grace of Allah-the largest infidel military force of the world was destroyed. And the myth of the super power was withered in front of the Mujahideen cries of Allahu Akbar (God is greater). Today we work from the same mountains to lift the iniquity that had been imposed on the Ummah by the Zionist-Crusader alliance, particularly after they have occupied the blessed land around Jerusalem, route of the journey of the Prophet (ALLAH'S BLESSING AND SALUTATIONS ON HIM) and the land of the two Holy Places. We ask Allah to bestow us with victory, He is our Patron and He is the Most Capable.

From here, today we begin the work, talking and discussing the ways of correcting what had happened to the Islamic world in general, and the Land of the two Holy Places in particular. We wish to study the means that we could follow to return the situation to its' normal path. And to return to the people their own rights, particularly after the large damages and the great aggression on the life and the religion of the people. An injustice that had affected every section and group of the people; the civilians, military and security men, government officials and merchants, the young and the old people as well as schools and university students.

Hundred of thousands of the unemployed graduates, who became the widest section of the society, were also affected.

Injustice had affected the people of the industry and agriculture. It affected the people of the rural and urban areas. And almost every body complain about something. The situation at the land of the two Holy places became like a huge volcano at the verge of eruption that would destroy the Kufr and the corruption and its' sources. The explosion at Riyadh and Al-Khobar is a warning of this volcanic eruption emerging as a result of the sever oppression, suffering, excessive iniquity, humiliation and poverty.

People are fully concerned about their every day livings; every body talks about the deterioration of the economy, inflation, ever increasing debts and jails full of prisoners. Government employees with limited income talk about debts of ten thousands and hundred thousands of Saudi Riyals . They complain that the value of the Riyal is greatly and continuously deteriorating among most of the main currencies. Great merchants and contractors speak about hundreds and thousands of million Riyals owed to them by the government. More than three hundred forty billions of Riyal owed by the government to the people in addition to the daily accumulated interest, let alone the foreign debt. People wonder whether we are the largest oil exporting country?! They even believe that this situation is a curse put on them by Allah for not objecting to the oppressive and illegitimate behaviour and measures of the ruling regime: Ignoring the divine Shari'ah law; depriving people of their legitimate rights; allowing the American to occupy the land of the two Holy Places; imprisonment, unjustly, of the sincere scholars. The honourable Ulamah and scholars as well as merchants, economists and eminent people of the country were all alerted by this disastrous situation.

Quick efforts were made by each group to contain and to correct the situation. All agreed that the country is heading toward a great catastrophe, the depth of which is not known except by Allah. One big merchant commented : " the king is leading the state into 'sixty-six' folded disaster", (We bemoan this and can only say: "No power and power acquiring except through Allah"). Numerous princes share with the people their feelings, privately expressing their concerns and objecting to the corruption, repression and the intimidation taking place in the country. But the competition between influential princes for personal gains and interest had destroyed the country. Through its course of actions the regime has torn off its legitimacy:

(1) Suspension of the Islamic Shari'ah law and exchanging it with man made civil law. The regime entered into a bloody confrontation with the truthful Ulamah and the righteous youths (we sanctify nobody; Allah sanctify Whom He pleaseth).

(2) The inability of the regime to protect the country, and allowing the enemy of the Ummah - the American crusader forces- to occupy the land for the longest of years. The crusader forces became the main cause of our disastrous condition, particularly in the economical aspect of it due to the unjustified heavy spending on these forces. As a result of the policy imposed on the country, especially in the field of oil industry where production is restricted or expanded and prices are fixed to suit the American economy ignoring the economy of the country. Expensive deals were imposed on the country to purchase arms. People asking what is the justification for the very existence of the regime then?

Quick efforts were made by individuals and by different groups of the society to contain the situation and to prevent the danger. They advised the government both privately and openly; they send letters and poems, reports after reports, reminders after reminders, they explored every avenue and enlist every influential man in their movement of reform and correction. They wrote with style of passion, diplomacy and wisdom asking for corrective measures and repentance from the "great wrong doings and corruption " that had engulfed even the basic principles of the religion and the legitimate rights of the people.

But -to our deepest regret- the regime refused to listen to the people accusing them of being ridiculous and imbecile. The matter got worse as previous wrong doings were followed by mischief's of greater magnitudes. All of this taking place in the land of the two Holy Places! It is no longer possible to be quiet. It is not acceptable to give a blind eye to this matter.

As the extent of these infringements reached the highest of levels and turned into demolishing forces threatening the very existence of the Islamic principles, a group of scholars-who can take no more-supported by hundreds of retired officials, merchants, prominent and educated people wrote to the King asking for implementation of the corrective measures. In 1411 A.H. (May 1991), at the time of the gulf war, a letter, the famous letter of Shawwaal, with over four hundred signatures was send to the king demanding the lift of oppression and the implementation of corrective actions. The king humiliated those people and choose to ignore the content of their letter; and the very bad situation of the country became even worse.

People, however, tried again and send more letters and petitions. One particular report, the glorious Memorandum Of Advice, was handed over to the king on Muharram, 1413 A.H (July 1992), which tackled the problem pointed out the illness and prescribed the medicine in an original, righteous and scientific style. It described the gaps and the shortcoming in the philosophy of the regime and suggested the required course of action and remedy. The report gave a description of:

(1) The intimidation and harassment suffered by the leaders of the society, the scholars, heads of tribes, merchants, academic teachers and other eminent individuals;

(2) The situation of the law within the country and the arbitrary declaration of what is Halal and Haram (lawful and unlawful) regardless of the Shari'ah as instituted by Allah;

(3) The state of the press and the media which became a tool of truth-hiding and misinformation; the media carried out the plan of the enemy of idolising cult of certain personalities and spreading scandals among the believers to repel the people away from their religion, as Allah, the Exalted said: {surely- as for- those who love that scandal should circulate between the believers, they shall have a grievous chastisement in this world and in the here after} (An-Noor, 24:19).

(4) Abuse and confiscation of human rights;

(5) The financial and the economical situation of the country and the frightening future in the view of the enormous amount of debts and interest owed by the government; this is at the time when the wealth of the Ummah being wasted to satisfy personal desires of certain individuals!! while imposing more custom duties and taxes on the nation. (the prophet said about the woman who committed adultery: "She repented in such a way sufficient to bring forgiveness to a custom collector!!").,

(6) The miserable situation of the social services and infra-structure especially the water service and supply , the basic requirement of life.,

(7) The state of the ill-trained and ill-prepared army and the impotence of its commander in chief despite the incredible amount of money that has been spent on the army. The gulf war clearly exposed the situation.,

(8) Shari'a law was suspended and man made law was used instead.,

(9) And as far as the foreign policy is concerned the report exposed not only how this policy has disregarded the Islamic issues and ignored the Muslims, but also how help and support were provided to the enemy against the Muslims; the cases of Gaza-Ariha and the communist in the south of Yemen are still fresh in the memory, and more can be said.

As stated by the people of knowledge, it is not a secret that to use man made law instead of the Shari'a and to support the infidels against the Muslims is one of the ten "voiders" that would strip a person from his Islamic status (turn a Muslim into a Mushrik, non believer status). The All Mighty said: {and whoever did not judge by what Allah revealed, those are the unbelievers} (Al-Ma'ida; 5:44), and {but no! by your Lord! they do not believe (in reality) until they make you a judge of that which has become a matter of disagreement among them, and then do not find the slightest misgiving in their hearts as to what you have decided and submit with entire submission} (An-Nissa; 4:65).

In spite of the fact that the report was written with soft words and very diplomatic style, reminding of Allah, giving truthful sincere advice, and despite of the importance of advice in Islam - being absolutely essential for those in charge of the people- and the large number who signed this document as well as their supporters, all of that was not an intercession for the Memorandum . Its' content was rejected and those who signed it and their sympathisers were ridiculed, prevented from travel, punished and even jailed.

Therefore it is very clear that the advocates of correction and reform movement were very keen on using peaceful means in order to protect the unity of the country and to prevent blood shed. Why is it then the regime closed all peaceful routes and pushed the people toward armed actions?!! which is the only choice left for them to implement righteousness and justice. To whose benefit does prince Sultan and prince Nayeff push the country into a civil war that will destroy everything? and why consulting those who ignites internal feuds, playing the people against each other and instigate the policemen, the sons of the nation, to abort the reform movement. While leaving in peace and security such traitors who implement the policy of the enemy in order to bleed the financial and the human resources of the Ummah, and leaving the main enemy in the area-the American Zionist alliance enjoy peace and security?!

The advisor (Zaki Badr, the Egyptian ex-minister of the interior) to prince Nayeff -minister of interior- was not acceptable even to his own country; he was sacked from his position there due to the filthy attitude and the aggression he exercised on his own people, yet he was warmly welcomed by prince Nayeff to assist in sins and aggressions. He unjustly filled the prisons with the best sons of this Ummah and caused miseries to their mothers. Does the regime want to play the civilians against their military personnel and vice versa, like what had happened in some of the neighbouring countries?!! No doubts this is the policy of the American-Israeli alliance as they are the first to benefit from this situation.

But with the grace of Allah, the majority of the nation, both civilians and military individuals are aware of the wicked plan. They refused to be played against each others and to be used by the regime as a tool to carry out the policy of the American-Israeli alliance through their agent in our country: the Saudi regime.

Therefore every one agreed that the situation can not be rectified (the shadow cannot be straighten when its' source, the rod, is not straight either) unless the root of the problem is tackled. Hence it is essential to hit the main enemy who divided the Ummah into small and little countries and pushed it, for the last few decades, into a state of confusion. The Zionist-Crusader alliance moves quickly to contain and abort any "corrective movement" appearing in the Islamic countries. Different means and methods are used to achieve their target; on occasion the "movement" is dragged into an armed struggle at a predetermined unfavourable time and place. Sometime officials from the Ministry of Interior, who are also graduates of the colleges of the Shari'ah, are leashed out to mislead and confuse the nation and the Ummah (by wrong *Fatwas*) and to circulate false information about the movement. At other occasions some righteous people were tricked into a war of words against the Ulama and the leaders of the movement, wasting the energy of the nation in discussing minor issues and ignoring the main one that is the unification of the people under the divine law of Allah.

In the shadow of these discussions and arguments truthfulness is covered by the falsehood, and personal feuds and partisanship created among the people increasing the division and the weakness of the Ummah; priorities of the Islamic work are lost while the blasphemy and polytheism continue its grip and control over the Ummah. We should be alert to these atrocious plans carried out by the Ministry of Interior. The right answer is to follow what have been decided by the people of knowledge, as was said by Ibn Taymiyyah (Allah's mercy upon him): "people of Islam should join forces and support each other to get rid of the main "Kufr" who is controlling the countries of the Islamic world, even to bear the lesser damage to get rid of the major one, that is the great Kufr".

If there are more than one duty to be carried out, then the most important one should receive priority. Clearly after Belief (Imaan) there is no more important duty than pushing the American enemy out of the holy land. No other priority, except Belief, could be considered before it; the people of knowledge, Ibn Taymiyyah, stated: "to fight in defence of religion and Belief is a collective duty; there is no other duty after Belief than fighting the enemy who is corrupting the life and the religion. There is no preconditions for this duty and the enemy should be fought with one best abilities. (ref: supplement of Fatwa). If it is not possible to push back the enemy except by the collective movement of the Muslim people, then there is a duty on the Muslims to ignore the minor differences among themselves; the ill effect of ignoring these differences, at a given period of time, is much less than the ill effect of the occupation of the Muslims' land by the main Kufr. Ibn Taymiyyah had explained this issue and emphasised the importance of dealing with the major threat on the expense of the minor one. He described the situation of the Muslims and the Mujahideen and stated that even the military personnel who are not practising Islam are not exempted from the duty of Jihad against the enemy.

Ibn Taymiyyah , after mentioning the Moguls (Tatar) and their behaviour in changing the law of Allah, stated that: the ultimate aim of pleasing Allah, raising His word, instituting His religion and obeying His messenger (ALLAH'S BLESSING AND SALUTATIONS ON HIM) is to fight the enemy, in every aspects and in a complete manner; if the danger to the religion from not fighting is greater than that of fighting, then it is a duty to fight them even if the intention of some of the fighter is not pure i.e . fighting for the sake of leadership (personal gain) or if they do not observe some of the rules and commandments of Islam. To repel the greatest of the two dangers on the expense of the lesser one is an Islamic principle which should be observed. It was the tradition of the people of the Sunnah (Ahlul-Sunnah) to join and invade- fight- with the righteous and non righteous men. Allah may support this religion by righteous and non righteous people as told by the prophet (ALLAH'S BLESSING AND SALUTATIONS ON HIM). If it is not possible to fight except with the help of non righteous military personnel and commanders, then there are two possibilities: either fighting will be ignored and the others, who are the great danger to this life and religion, will take control; or to fight with the help of non righteous rulers and therefore repelling the greatest of the two dangers and implementing most, though not all, of the Islamic laws. The latter option is the right duty to be carried out in these circumstances and in many other similar situation. In fact many of the fights and conquests that took place after the time of Rashidoon, the guided Imams, were of this type. (majmoo' al Fatwa, 26/506).

No one, not even a blind or a deaf person , can deny the presence of the widely spread mischief's or the prevalence of the great sins that had reached the grievous iniquity of polytheism and to share with Allah in His sole right of sovereignty and making of the law. The All Mighty stated: {And when Luqman said to his son while he admonish him: O my son! do not associate ought with Allah; most surely polytheism is a grievous iniquity} (Luqman; 31:13). Man fabricated laws were put forward permitting what has been forbidden by Allah such as usury (Riba) and other matters. Banks dealing in usury are competing, for lands, with the two Holy Places and declaring war against Allah by disobeying His order {Allah has allowed trading and forbidden usury} (Baqarah; 2:275). All this taking place at the vicinity of the Holy Mosque in the Holy Land! Allah (SWT) stated in His Holy Book a unique promise (that had not been promised to any other sinner) to the Muslims who deals in usury: {O you who believe! Be careful of your duty to Allah and relinquish what remains (due) from usury, if you are believers * But if you do (it) not, then be appraised of WAR from Allah and His Apostle} (Baqarah; 2:278-279). This is for the "Muslim" who deals in usury (believing that it is a sin), what is it then to the person who make himself a partner and equal to Allah, legalising (usury and other sins) what has been forbidden by Allah. Despite of all of the above we see the government misled and dragged some of the righteous Ulamah and Da'ees away from the issue of objecting to the greatest of sins and Kufr. (We bemoan this and can only say: "No power and power acquiring except through Allah").

Under such circumstances, to push the enemy-the greatest Kufr-out of the country is a prime duty. No other duty after Belief is more important than the duty of had . Utmost effort should be made to prepare and instigate the Ummah against the enemy, the American-Israeli alliance- occupying the country of the two Holy Places and the route of the Apostle (Allah's Blessings and Salutations may be on him) to the Furthest Mosque (Al-Aqsa Mosque). Also to remind the Muslims not to be engaged in an internal war among themselves, as that will have grieve consequences namely:

1-consumption of the Muslims human resources as most casualties and fatalities will be among the Muslims people.

2-Exhaustion of the economic and financial resources.

3-Destruction of the country infrastructures

4-Dissociation of the society

5-Destruction of the oil industries. The presence of the USA Crusader military forces on land, sea and air of the states of the Islamic Gulf is the greatest danger threatening the largest oil reserve in the world. The existence of these forces in the area will provoke the people of the country and induces aggression on their religion, feelings and prides and push them to take up armed struggle against the invaders occupying the land; therefore spread of the fighting in the region will expose the oil wealth to the danger of being burned up. The economic interests of the States of the Gulf and the land of the two Holy Places will be damaged and even a greater damage will be caused to the economy of the world. I would like here to alert my brothers, the Mujahideen, the sons of the nation, to protect this (oil) wealth and not to include it in the battle as it is a great Islamic wealth and a large economical power essential for the soon to be established Islamic state, by Allah's Permission and Grace. We also warn the aggressors, the USA, against burning this Islamic wealth (a crime which they may commit in order to prevent it, at the end of the war, from falling in the hands of its legitimate owners and to cause economic damages to the competitors of the USA in Europe or the Far East, particularly Japan which is the major consumer of the oil of the region).

6-Division of the land of the two Holy Places, and annexing of the northerly part of it by Israel. Dividing the land of the two Holy Places is an essential demand of the Zionist-Crusader alliance. The existence of such a large country with its huge resources under the leadership of the forthcoming Islamic State, by Allah's Grace, represent a serious danger to the very existence of the Zionist state in Palestine. The Nobel Ka'ba, -the Qiblah of all Muslims- makes the land of the two Holy Places a symbol for the unity of the Islamic world. Moreover, the presence of the world largest oil reserve makes the land of the two Holy Places an important economical power in the Islamic world. The sons of the two Holy Places are directly related to the life style (Seerah) of their forefathers, the companions, may Allah be pleased with them. They consider the Seerah of their forefathers as a source and an example for re-establishing the greatness of this Ummah and to raise the word of Allah again. Furthermore the presence of a population of fighters in the south of Yemen, fighting in the cause of Allah, is a strategic threat to the Zionist-Crusader alliance in the area. The Prophet (ALLAH'S BLESSING AND SALUTATIONS ON HIM) said: (around twelve thousands will emerge from Aden/Abian helping -the cause of- Allah and His messenger, they are the best, in the time, between me and them) narrated by Ahmad with a correct trustworthy reference.

7-An internal war is a great mistake, no matter what reasons are there for it. the presence of the occupier-the USA- forces will control the outcome of the battle for the benefit of the international Kufr.

I address now my brothers of the security and military forces and the national guards may Allah preserve you hoard for Islam and the Muslims people:

O you protectors of unity and guardians of Faith; O you descendent of the ancestors who carried the light (torch) of guidance and spread it all over the world. O you grandsons of Sa'd Ibn Abi Waqqaas, Almothanna Ibn Haritha Ash-Shaybani, Alga'ga' Ibn Amroo Al-Tameemi and those pious companions who fought Jihad alongside them; you competed to join the army and the guard forces with the intention to carry out Jihad in the cause of Allah -raising His word- and to defend the faith of Islam and the land of the two Holy Places against the invaders and the occupying forces. That is the ultimate level of believing in this religion "Deen". But the regime had reversed these principles and their understanding, humiliating the Ummah and disobeying Allah. Half a century ago the rulers promised the Ummah to regain the first Qiblah, but fifty years later new generation arrived and the promises have been changed; Al-Aqsa Mosque handed over to the Zionists and the wounds of the Ummah still bleeding there. At the time when the Ummah has not regained the first Qiblah and the rout of the journey of the Prophet (Allah's Blessings and Salutations may be on him), and despite of all of the above, the Saudi regime had stunt the Ummah in the remaining sanctities, the Holy city of Makka and the mosque of the Prophet (Al-Masjid An-Nabawy), by calling the Christians army to defend the regime. The crusaders were permitted to be in the land of the two Holy Places. Not surprisingly though, the King himself wore the cross on his chest. The country was widely opened from the north-to- the south and from east-to-the west for the crusaders. The land was filled with the military bases of the USA and the allies. The regime became unable to keep control without the help of these bases. You know more than any body else about the size, intention and the danger of the presence of the USA military bases in the area. The regime betrayed the Ummah and joined the Kufr, assisting and helping them against the Muslims. It is well known that this is one of the ten "voiders" of Islam, deeds of de-Islamisation. By opening the Arab peninsula to the crusaders the regime disobeyed and acted against what has been enjoined by the messenger of Allah (Allah's Blessings and Salutations may be on him), while he was at the bed of his death: (Expel the polytheists out of the Arab Peninsula); (narrated by Al-Bukhari) and: (If I survive, Allah willing, I'll expel the Jews and the Christians out of the Arab Peninsula); saheeh Aljame' As-Sagheer.

It is out of date and no longer acceptable to claim that the presence of the crusaders is necessity and only a temporary measures to protect the land of the two Holy Places. Especially when the civil and the military infrastructures of Iraq were savagely destroyed showing the depth of the Zionist-Crusaders hatred to the Muslims and their children, and the rejection of the idea of replacing the crusaders forces by an Islamic force composed of the sons of the country and other Muslim people. moreover the foundations of the claim and the claim it self were demolished and wiped out by the sequence of speeches given by the leaders of the Kuffar in America. The latest of these speeches was the one given by William Perry, the Defense Secretary, after the explosion in Al-Khobar saying that: the presence of the American solders there is to protect the interest of the USA. The imprisoned Sheikh Safar Al-Hawali, may Allah hasten his release, wrote a book of seventy pages; in it he presented evidence and proof that the presence of the Americans in the Arab Peninsula is a pre-planed military occupation. The regime want to deceive the Muslim people in the same manner when the Palestinian fighters, Mujahideen, were deceived causing the loss of Al-Aqsa Mosque. In 1304 A.H (1936 AD) the awakened Muslims nation of Palestine started their great struggle, Jihad, against the British occupying forces. Britain was impotent to stop the Mujahideen and their Jihad, but their devil inspired that there is no way to stop the armed struggle in Palestine unless through their agent King Abdul Azeez, who managed to deceives the Mujahideen. King Abdul Azeez carried out his duty to his British masters. He sent his two sons to meet the Mujahideen leaders and to inform them that King Abdul Azeez would guarantee the promises made by the British government in leaving the area and responding positively to the demands of the Mujahideen if the latter stop their Jihad. And so King Abdul Azeez caused the loss of the first Qiblah of the Muslims people. The King joined the crusaders against the Muslims and instead of supporting the Mujahideen in the cause of Allah, to liberate the Al-Aqsa Mosque, he disappointed and humiliated them.

Today, his son, king Fahd, trying to deceive the Muslims for the second time so as to loose what is left of the sancticies. When the Islamic world resented the arrival of the crusader forces to the land of the two Holy Places, the king told lies to the Ulamah (who issued *Fatwas* about the arrival of the Americans) and to the gathering of the Islamic leaders at the conference of Rabitah which was held in the Holy City of Makka. The King said that: "the issue is simple, the American and the alliance forces will leave the area in few months". Today it is seven years since their arrival and the regime is not able to move them out of the country. The regime made no confession about its inability and carried on lying to the people claiming that the American will leave. But never-never again ; a believer will not be bitten twice from the same hole or snake! Happy is the one who takes note of the sad experience of the others!!

Instead of motivating the army, the guards, and the security men to oppose the occupiers, the regime used these men to protect the invaders, and further deepening the humiliation and the betrayal. (We bemoan this and can only say: "No power and power acquiring except through Allah"). To those little group of men within the army, police and security forces, who have been tricked and pressured by the regime to attack the Muslims and spill their blood, we would like to remind them of the narration: (I promise war against those who take my friends as their enemy) narrated by Al--Bukhari. And his saying (Allah's Blessings and Salutations may be on him) saying of: (In the day of judgement a man comes holding another and complaining being slain by him. Allah, blessed be His Names, asks: Why did you slay him?! The accused replies: I did so that all exaltation may be Yours. Allah, blessed be His Names, says: All exaltation is indeed mine! Another man comes holding a fourth with a similar complaint. Allah, blessed be His Names, asks: Why did you kill him?! The accused replies: I did so that exaltation may be for Mr. X! Allah, blessed be His Names, says: exaltation is mine, not for Mr. X, carry all the slain man's sins (and proceed to the Hell fire)!). In another wording of An-Nasa'i: "The accused says: for strengthening the rule or kingdom of Mr. X"

Today your brothers and sons, the sons of the two Holy Places, have started their Jihad in the cause of Allah, to expel the occupying enemy from of the country of the two Holy places. And there is no doubt you would like to carry out this mission too, in order to re-establish the greatness of this Ummah and to liberate its' occupied sanctities. Nevertheless, it must be obvious to you that, due to the imbalance of power between our armed forces and the enemy forces, a suitable means of fighting must be adopted i.e using fast moving light forces that work under complete secrecy. In other word to initiate a guerrilla warfare, were the sons of the nation, and not the military forces, take part in it. And as you know, it is wise, in the present circumstances, for the armed military forces not to be engaged in a conventional fighting with the forces of the crusader enemy (the exceptions are the bold and the forceful operations carried out by the members of the armed forces individually, that is without the movement of the formal forces in its conventional shape and hence the responses will not be directed, strongly, against the army) unless a big advantage is likely to be achieved; and great losses induced on the enemy side (that would shaken and destroy its foundations and infrastructures) that will help to expel the defeated enemy from the country.

The Mujahideen, your brothers and sons, requesting that you support them in every possible way by supplying them with the necessary information, materials and arms. Security men are especially asked to cover up for the Mujahideen and to assist them as much as possible against the occupying enemy; and to spread rumours, fear and discouragement among the members of the enemy forces.

We bring to your attention that the regime, in order to create a friction and feud between the Mujahideen and yourselves, might resort to take a deliberate action against personnel of the security, guards and military forces and blame the Mujahideen for these actions. The regime should not be allowed to have such opportunity.

The regime is fully responsible for what had been incurred by the country and the nation; however the occupying American enemy is the principle and the main cause of the situation . Therefore efforts should be concentrated on destroying, fighting and killing the enemy until, by the Grace of Allah, it is completely defeated. The time will come -by the Permission of Allah- when you'll perform your decisive role so that the word of Allah will be supreme and the word of the infidels (Kaferoon) will be the inferior. You will hit with iron fist against the aggressors. You'll re-establish the normal course and give the people their rights and carry out your truly Islamic duty. Allah willing, I'll have a separate talk about these issues.

My Muslim Brothers (particularly those of the Arab Peninsula): The money you pay to buy American goods will be transformed into bullets and used against our brothers in Palestine and tomorrow (future) against our sons in the land of the two Holy places. By buying these goods we are strengthening their economy while our dispossession and poverty increases.

Muslims Brothers of land of the two Holy Places:

It is incredible that our country is the world largest buyer of arms from the USA and the area biggest commercial partners of the Americans who are assisting their Zionist brothers in occupying Palestine and in evicting and killing the Muslims there, by providing arms, men and financial supports.

To deny these occupiers from the enormous revenues of their trading with our country is a very important help for our Jihad against them. To express our anger and hate to them is a very important moral gesture. By doing so we would have taken part in (the process of) cleansing our sanctities from the crusaders and the Zionists and forcing them, by the Permission of Allah, to leave disappointed and defeated.

We expect the woman of the land of the two Holy Places and other countries to carry out their role in boycotting the American goods.

If economical boycotting is intertwined with the military operations of the Mujahideen, then defeating the enemy will be even nearer, by the Permission of Allah. However if Muslims don't co-operate and support their Mujahideen brothers then , in effect, they are supplying the army of the enemy with financial help and extending the war and increasing the suffering of the Muslims.

The security and the intelligence services of the entire world can not force a single citizen to buy the goods of his/her enemy. Economical boycotting of the American goods is a very effective weapon of hitting and weakening the enemy, and it is not under the control of the security forces of the regime.

Before closing my talk, I have a very important message to the youths of Islam, men of the brilliant future of the Ummah of Muhammad (ALLAH'S BLESSING AND SALUTATIONS ON HIM). Our talk with the youths about their duty in this difficult period in the history of our Ummah. A period in which the youths and no one else came forward to carry out the variable and different duties. While some of the well known individuals had hesitated in their duty of defending Islam and saving themselves and their wealth from the injustice, aggression and terror -exercised by the government- the youths (may Allah protect them) were forthcoming and raised the banner of Jihad against the American-Zionist alliance occupying the sanctities of Islam. Others who have been tricked into loving this materialistic world, and those who have been terrorised by the government choose to give legitimacy to the greatest betrayal , the occupation of the land of the two Holy Places (We bemoan this and can only say: "No power and power acquiring except through Allah"). We are not surprised from the action of our youths. The youths were the companions of Muhammad (Allah's Blessings and Salutations may be on him), and was it not the youths themselves who killed Aba-Jahl, the Pharaoh of this Ummah? Our youths are the best descendent of the best ancestors.

Abdul-Rahman Ibn Awf -may Allah be pleased with him- said: (I was at Badr where I noticed two youths one to my right and the other to my left. One of them asked me quietly (so not to be heard by the other) : O uncle point out Aba-Jahl to me. What do you want him for? , said Abdul Rahman. The boy answered: I have been informed that he- Aba-Jahl- abused the Messenger of Allah (), I swear by Allah, who have my soul in His hand, that if I see Aba-Jahl I'll not let my shadow departs his shadow till one of us is dead. I was astonished, said Abdul Rahman; then the other youth said the same thing as the first one. Subsequently I saw Aba-Jahl among the people; I said to the boys do you see? this is the man you are asking me about. The two youths hit Aba-Jahl with their swords till he was dead. Allah is the greatest, Praise be to Him: Two youths of young age but with great perseverance, enthusiasm, courage and pride for the religion of Allah's, each one of them asking about the most important act of killing that should be induced on the enemy. That is the killing of the pharaoh of this Ummah - Aba Jahl-, the leader of the unbelievers (Mushrikeen) at the battle of Badr. The role of Abdul Rahman Ibn Awf , may Allah be pleased with him, was to direct the two youths toward Aba-Jahl. That was the perseverance and the enthusiasm of the youths of that time and that was the perseverance and the enthusiasm of their fathers. It is this role that is now required from the people who have the expertise and knowledge in fighting the enemy. They should guide their brothers and sons in this matter; once that has been done, then our youths will repeat what their forefathers had said before: "I swear by Allah if I see him I'll not let my shadow to departs from his shadow till one of us is dead".

And the story of Abdur-Rahman Ibn Awf about Ummayyah Ibn Khalaf shows the extent of Bilal's (may Allah be pleased with him) persistence in killing the head of the Kufr: "the head of Kufr is Ummayyah Ibn Khalaf.... I shall live not if he survives" said Bilal.

Few days ago the news agencies had reported that the Defence Secretary of the Crusading Americans had said that "the explosion at Riyadh and Al-Khobar had taught him one lesson: that is not to withdraw when attacked by coward terrorists".

We say to the Defence Secretary that his talk can induce a grieving mother to laughter! and shows the fears that had enshrined you all. Where was this false courage of yours when the explosion in Beirut took place on 1983 AD (1403 A.H). You were turned into scattered pits and pieces at that time; 241 mainly marines solders were killed. And where was this courage of yours when two explosions made you to leave Aden in lees than twenty four hours!

But your most disgraceful case was in Somalia; where- after vigorous propaganda about the power of the USA and its post cold war leadership of the new world order- you moved tens of thousands of international force, including twenty eight thousands American solders into Somalia. However, when tens of your solders were killed in minor battles and one American Pilot was dragged in the streets of Mogadishu you left the area carrying disappointment, humiliation, defeat and your dead with you. Clinton appeared in front of the whole world threatening and promising revenge , but these threats were merely a preparation for withdrawal. You have been disgraced by Allah and you withdrew; the extent of your impotence and weaknesses became very clear. It was a pleasure for the "heart" of every Muslim and a remedy to the "chests" of believing nations to see you defeated in the three Islamic cities of Beirut , Aden and Mogadishu.

I say to Secretary of Defence: The sons of the land of the two Holy Places had come out to fight against the Russian in Afghanistan, the Serb in Bosnia-Herzegovina and today they are fighting in Chechenia and -by the Permission of Allah- they have been made victorious over your partner, the Russians. By the command of Allah, they are also fighting in Tajakistan.

I say: Since the sons of the land of the two Holy Places feel and strongly believe that fighting (Jihad) against the Kuffar in every part of the world, is absolutely essential; then they would be even more enthusiastic, more powerful and larger in number upon fighting on their own land- the place of their births- defending the greatest of their sanctities, the noble Ka'ba (the Qiblah of all Muslims). They know that the Muslims of the world will assist and help them to victory. To liberate their sanctities is the greatest of issues concerning all Muslims; It is the duty of every Muslims in this world.

I say to you William (Defence Secretary) that: These youths love death as you loves life. They inherit dignity, pride, courage, generosity, truthfulness and sacrifice from father to father. They are most delivering and steadfast at war. They inherit these values from their ancestors (even from the time of the Jaheliyyah, before Islam). These values were approved and completed by the arriving Islam as stated by the messenger of Allah (Allah's Blessings and Salutations may be on him): "I have been send to perfecting the good values". (Saheeh Al-Jame' As-Sagheer).

When the pagan King Amroo Ibn Hind tried to humiliate the pagan Amroo Ibn Kulthoom, the latter cut the head of the King with his sword rejecting aggression, humiliation and indignation.

If the king oppresses the people excessively, we reject submitting to humiliation.

By which legitimacy (or command) O Amroo bin Hind you want us to be degraded?!

By which legitimacy (or command) O Amroo bin Hind you listen to our foes and disrespect us?!

Our toughness has, O Amroo, tired the enemies before you, never giving in!

Our youths believe in paradise after death. They believe that taking part in fighting will not bring their day nearer; and staying behind will not postpone their day either. Exalted be to Allah who said: {And a soul will not die but with the permission of Allah, the term is fixed} (Aal Imraan; 3:145). Our youths believe in the saying of the messenger of Allah (Allah's Blessings and Salutations may be on him): "O boy, I teach a few words; guard (guard the cause of, keep the commandments of) Allah, then He guards you, guard (the cause of) Allah, then He will be with you; if you ask (for your need) ask Allah, if you seek assistance, seek Allah's; and know definitely that if the Whole World gathered to (bestow) profit on you they will not profit you except with what was determined for you by Allah, and if they gathered to harm you they will not harm you except with what has been determined for you by Allah; Pen lifted, papers dried, it is fixed nothing in these truths can be changed" Saheeh Al-Jame' As-Sagheer. Our youths took note of the meaning of the poetic verse:

"If death is a predetermined must, then it is a shame to die cowardly." and the other poet saying: "Who do not die by the sword will die by other reason; many causes are there but one death".

These youths believe in what has been told by Allah and His messenger (Allah's Blessings and Salutations may be on him) about the greatness of the reward for the Mujahideen and Martyrs; Allah, the most exalted said: {and -so far- those who are slain in the way of Allah, He will by no means allow their deeds to perish. He will guide them and improve their condition. and cause them to enter the garden -paradise- which He has made known to them}. (Muhammad; 47:4-6). Allah the Exalted also said: {and do not speak of those who are slain in Allah's way as dead; nay -they are- alive, but you do not perceive} (Bagarah; 2:154). His messenger (Allah's Blessings and Salutations may be on him) said: "for those who strive in His cause Allah prepared hundred degrees (levels) in paradise; in-between two degrees as the in-between heaven and earth". Saheeh Al-Jame' As-Sagheer. He (Allah's Blessings and Salutations may be on him) also said: "the best of the martyrs are those who do NOT turn their faces away from the battle till they are killed. They are in the high level of Jannah (paradise). Their Lord laughs to them (in pleasure) and when your Lord laughs to a slave of His, He will not hold him to an account". narrated by Ahmad with correct and trustworthy reference. And : "a martyr will not feel the pain of death except like how you feel when you are pinched". Saheeh Al-Jame' As-Sagheer. He also said: "a martyr privileges are guaranteed by Allah; forgiveness with the first gush of his blood, he will be shown his seat in paradise, he will be decorated with the jewels of belief (Imaan), married off to the beautiful ones, protected from the test in the grave, assured security in the day of judgement, crowned with the crown of dignity, a ruby of which is better than this whole world (Duniah) and its' entire content, wedded to seventy two of the pure Houries (beautiful ones of Paradise) and his intercession on the behalf of seventy of his relatives will be accepted". Narrated by Ahmad and At-Tirmithi (with the correct and trustworthy reference).

Those youths know that their rewards in fighting you, the USA, is double than their rewards in fighting some one else not from the people of the book. They have no intention except to enter paradise by killing you. An infidel, and enemy of God like you, cannot be in the same hell with his righteous executioner.

Our youths chanting and reciting the word of Allah, the most exalted: {fight them; Allah will punish them by your hands and bring them to disgrace, and assist you against them and heal the heart of a believing people} (At-Taubah; 9:14) and the words of the prophet (ALLAH'S BLESSING AND SALUTATIONS ON HIM): "I swear by Him, who has my soul in His hand, that no man get killed fighting them today, patiently attacking and not retreating ,surely Allah will let him into paradise". And his (Allah's Blessings and Salutations may be on him) saying to them: "get up to a paradise as wide as heaven and earth".

The youths also reciting the All Mighty words of: "so when you meat in battle those who disbelieve, then smite the necks..." (Muhammad; 47:19). Those youths will not ask you (William Perry) for explanations, they will tell you singing there is nothing between us need to be explained, there is only killing and neck smiting.

And they will say to you what their grand father, Haroon Ar-Rasheed, Ameer-ul-Mu'meneen, replied to your grandfather, Nagfoor, the Byzantine emperor, when he threatened the Muslims: "from Haroon Ar-Rasheed, Ameer-ul-Mu'meneen, to Nagfoor, the dog of the Romans; the answer is what you will see not what you hear". Haroon El-Rasheed led the armies of Islam to the battle and handed Nagfoor a devastating defeat.

The youths you called cowards are competing among themselves for fighting and killing you. reciting what one of them said: The crusader army became dust when we detonated al-Khobar. With courageous youth of Islam fearing no danger. If (they are) threatened: The tyrants will kill you, they reply my death is a victory. I did not betray that king, he did betray our Qiblah. And he permitted in the holy country the most filthy sort of humans. I have made an oath by Allah, the Great, to fight who ever rejected the faith. For more than a decade, they carried arms on their shoulders in Afghanistan and they have made vows to Allah that as long as they are alive, they will continue to carry arms against you until you are -Allah willing- expelled, defeated and humiliated, they will carry on as long as they live saying: O William, tomorrow you will know which young man is confronting your misguided brethren! A youth fighting in smile, returning with the spear coloured red. May Allah keep me close to knights, humans in peace, demons in war. Lions in Jungle but their teeth are spears and Indian swords. The horses witness that I push them hard forwarded in the fire of battle.

The dust of the battle bears witnesses for me, so also the fighting itself, the pens and the books!

So to abuse the grandsons of the companions, may Allah be pleased with them, by calling them cowards and challenging them by refusing to leave the land of the two Holy Places shows the insanity and the imbalance you are suffering from. Its appropriate "remedy," however, is in the hands of the youths of Islam, as the poet said:

I am willing to sacrifice self and wealth for knights who never disappointed me.

Knights who are never fed up or deterred by death, even if the mill of war turns.

In the heat of battle they do not care, and cure the insanity of the enemy by their 'insane' courage.

Terrorising you, while you are carrying arms on our land, is a legitimate and morally demanded duty. It is a legitimate right well known to all humans and other creatures. Your example and our example is like a snake which entered into a house of a man and got killed by him. The coward is the one who lets you walk, while carrying arms, freely on his land and provides you with peace and security.

Those youths are different from your soldiers. Your problem will be how to convince your troops to fight, while our problem will be how to restrain our youths to wait for their turn in fighting and in operations. These youths are commendation and praiseworthy.

They stood up tall to defend the religion; at the time when the government misled the prominent scholars and tricked them into issuing *Fatwas* (that have no basis neither in the book of Allah, nor in the Sunnah of His prophet (Allah's Blessings and Salutations may be on him)) of opening the land of the two Holy Places for the Christians armies and handing the Al-Aqsa Mosque to the Zionists. Twisting the meanings of the holy text will not change this fact at all. They deserve the praise of the poet: I rejected all the critics, who chose the wrong way; I rejected those who enjoy fireplaces in clubs discussing eternally; I rejected those, who inspite being lost, think they are at the goal; I respect those who carried on not asking or bothering about the difficulties; Never letting up from their goals, inspite all hardships of the road; Whose blood is the oil for the flame guiding in the darkness of confusion; I feel still the pain of (the loss) Al-Quds in my internal organs; That loss is like a burning fire in my intestines; I did not betray my covenant with God, when even states did betray it! As their grandfather Assim Bin Thabit said rejecting a surrender offer of the pagans:

What for an excuse I had to surrender, while I am still able, having arrows and my bow having a tough string?!

Death is truth and ultimate destiny, and life will end any way. If I do not fight you, then my mother must be insane!

The youths hold you responsible for all of the killings and evictions of the Muslims and the violation of the sanctities, carried out by your Zionist brothers in Lebanon; you openly supplied them with arms and finance. More than 600,000 Iraqi children have died due to lack of food and medicine and as a result of the unjustifiable aggression (sanction) imposed on Iraq and its nation. The children of Iraq are our children. You, the USA, together with the Saudi regime are responsible for the shedding of the blood of these innocent children. Due to all of that, what ever treaty you have with our country is now null and void.

The treaty of Hudaybiyyah was cancelled by the messenger of Allah (Allah's Blessings and Salutations may be on him) once Quraysh had assisted Bani Bakr against Khusa'ah, the allies of the prophet (Allah's Blessings and Salutations may be on him). The prophet (Allah's Blessings and Salutations may be on him) fought Quraysh and concurred Makka. He (Allah's Blessings and Salutations may be on him) considered the treaty with Bani Qainuqa' void because one of their Jews publicy hurt one Muslim woman, one single woman, at the market. Let alone then, the killing you caused to hundred of thousands Muslims and occupying their sanctities. It is now clear that those who claim that the blood of the American solders (the enemy occupying the land of the Muslims) should be protected are merely repeating what is imposed on them by the regime; fearing the aggression and interested in saving themselves. It is a duty now on every tribe in the Arab Peninsula to fight, Jihad, in the cause of Allah and to cleanse the land from those occupiers. Allah knows that there blood is permitted (to be spilled) and their wealth is a booty; their wealth is a booty to those who kill them. The most Exalted said in the verse of As-Sayef, The Sword: "so when the sacred months have passed away, then slay the idolaters where ever you find them, and take them captives and besiege them and lie in wait for them in every ambush" (At-Tauba; 9:5). Our youths knew that the humiliation suffered by the Muslims as a result of the occupation of their sanctities can not be kicked and removed except by explosions and Jihad. As the poet said:

The walls of oppression and humiliation cannot be demolished except in a rain of bullets.

The freeman does not surrender leadership to infidels and sinners.

Without shedding blood no degradation and branding can be removed from the forehead.

I remind the youths of the Islamic world, who fought in Afghanistan and Bosnia-Herzegovina with their wealth, pens, tongues and themselves that the battle had not finished yet. I remind them about the talk between Jibreel (Gabriel) and the messenger of Allah (Allah's Blessings and Salutations may be on both of them) after the battle of Ahzab when the messenger of Allah (Allah's Blessings and Salutations may be on him) returned to Medina and before putting his sword aside; when Jibreel (Allah's Blessings and Salutations may be on him) descend saying: "are you putting your sword aside? by Allah the angels haven't dropped their arms yet; march with your companions to Bani Quraydah, I am (going) ahead of you to throw fears in their hearts and to shake their fortresses on them". Jibreel marched with the angels (Allah's Blessings and Salutations may be on them all), followed by the messenger of Allah (Allah's Blessings and Salutations may be on him) marching with the immigrants, Muhajeroon, and supporters, Ansar. (narrated by Al-Bukhary).

These youths know that: if one is not to be killed one will die (any way) and the most honourable death is to be killed in the way of Allah. They are even more determined after the martyrdom of the four heroes who bombed the Americans in Riyadh. Those youths who raised high the head of the Ummah and humiliated the Americans-the occupier-by their operation in Riyadh. They remember the poetry of Ja'far, the second commander in the battle of Mu'tah, in which three thousand Muslims faced over a hundred thousand Romans:

How good is the Paradise and its nearness, good with cool drink But the Romans are promised punishment (in Hell), if I meet them.

I will fight them.

And the poetry of Abdullah Bin Rawaha, the third commander in the battle of Mu'tah, after the martyrdom of Ja'far, when he felt some hesitation:

O my soul if you do not get killed, you are going to die, anyway.

This is death pool in front of you!

You are getting what you have wished for (martyrdom) before, and you follow the example of the two previous commanders you are rightly guided!

As for our daughters, wives, sisters and mothers they should take prime example from the prophet (Allah's Blessings and Salutations may be on him) pious female companions, may Allah be pleased with them; they should adopt the life style (Seerah) of the female companions of courage, sacrifice and generosity in the cause of the supremacy of Allah's religion.

They should remember the courage and the personality of Fatima, daughter of Khatab, when she accepted Islam and stood up in front of her brother, Omar Ibn Al-Khatab and challenged him (before he became a Muslim) saying: "O Omar , what will you do if the truth is not in your religion?!" And to remember the stand of Asma', daughter of Abu Bakr, on the day of Hijra, when she attended the Messenger and his companion in the cave and split her belt in two pieces for them. And to remember the stand of Naseeba Bent Ka'b striving to defend the messenger of Allah (Allah's Blessings and Salutations may be on him) on the day of Uhud, in which she suffered twelve injuries, one of which was so deep leaving a deep lifelong scar! They should remember the generosity of the early woman of Islam who raised finance for the Muslims army by selling their jewelery.

Our women had set a tremendous example of generosity in the cause of Allah; they motivated and encouraged their sons, brothers and husbands to fight- in the cause of Allah- in Afghanistan, Bosnia-Herzegovina, Chechenia and in other countries. We ask Allah to accept from them these deeds, and may He help their fathers, brothers, husbands and sons. May Allah strengthen the belief - Imaan - of our women in the way of generosity and sacrifice for the supremacy of the word of Allah. Our women weep not, except over men who fight in the cause of Allah; our women instigate their brothers to fight in the cause of Allah.

Our women bemoan only fighters in the cause of Allah, as said: Do not moan on any one except a lion in the woods, courageous in the burning wars. Let me die dignified in wars, honourable death is better than my current life.

Our women encourage Jihad saying: Prepare yourself like a struggler, the matter is bigger than words! Are you going to leave us else for the wolves of Kufr eating our wings?! The wolves of Kufr are mobilising all evil persons from every where! Where are the freemen defending free women by the arms?! Death is better than life in humiliation! Some scandals and shames will never be otherwise eradicated.

My Muslim Brothers of The World: Your brothers in Palestine and in the land of the two Holy Places are calling upon your help and asking you to take part in fighting against the enemy --your enemy and their enemy-- the Americans and the Israelis. they are asking you to do whatever you can, with one own means and ability, to expel the enemy, humiliated and defeated, out of the sanctities of Islam. Exalted be to

Allah said in His book: { and if they ask your support, because they are oppressed in their faith, then support them!} (Anfaal; 8:72)

O you horses (soldiers) of Allah ride and march on. This is the time of hardship so be tough. And know that your gathering and co-operation in order to liberate the sanctities of Islam is the right step toward unifying the word of the Ummah under the banner of "No God but Allah").

From our place we raise our palms humbly to Allah asking Him to bestow on us His guide in every aspects of this issue.

Our Lord, we ask you to secure the release of the truthful scholars, Ulama, of Islam and pious youths of the Ummah from their imprisonment. O Allah, strengthen them and help their families.

Our Lord, the people of the cross had come with their horses (soldiers) and occupied the land of the two Holy places. And the Zionist Jews fiddling as they wish with the Al-Aqsa Mosque, the route of the ascendance of the messenger of Allah (ALLAH'S BLESSING AND SALUTATIONS ON HIM). Our Lord, shatter their gathering, divide them among themselves, shaken the earth under their feet and give us control over them; Our Lord, we take refuge in you from their deeds and take you as a shield between us and them

Our Lord, show us a black day in them!

Our Lord, show us the wonderment of your ability in them!

Our Lord, You are the Revealer of the book, Director of the clouds, You defeated the allies (Ahzab); defeat them and make us victorious over them.

Our Lord, You are the one who help us and You are the one who assist us, with Your Power we move and by Your Power we fight. On You we rely and You are our cause.

Our Lord, those youths got together to make Your religion victorious and raise Your banner. Our Lord, send them Your help and strengthen their hearts.

Our Lord, make the youths of Islam steadfast and descend patience on them and guide their shots!

Our Lord, unify the Muslims and bestow love among their hearts!

O Lord pour down upon us patience, and make our steps firm and assist us against the unbelieving people!

Our Lord, do not lay on us a burden as Thou didst lay on those before us; Our Lord, do not impose upon us that which we have no strength to bear; and pardon us and grant us protection and have mercy on us, Thou art our patron, so help us against the unbelieving people.

Our Lord, guide this Ummah, and make the right conditions (by which) the people of your obedience will be in dignity and the people of disobedience in humiliation, and by which the good deeds are enjoined and the bad deeds are forebode.

Our Lord, bless Muhammad, Your slave and messenger, his family and descendants, and companions and salute him with a (becoming) salutation.

And our last supplication is: All praise is due to Allah."

In 1998, bin Laden reissued his earlier Fatwa. The key statement within this declaration was for, "[A]ll Muslims: the ruling to kill the Americans and their allies – civilians and military – is an individual duty for every Muslim who can do it in any country in which it is possible to do it."[64] Magnus Ranstorp, from St. Andrews University, concludes that:

"The primary core issue for Islamists in general has been the recapture of the al-Aqsa mosque in Jerusalem and the destruction of the artificially created state, Israel . . . Bin-Laden continuously refers to a Judeo-Christian alliance and links the situations in Israel and Saudi Arabia to a phased plan to de-Islamicize and occupy Islam's sacred land and places everywhere . . . The fatwa thus is an auxiliary tool to mobilize support among followers and sympathizers as well as to inspire and exploit fear in the enemy."[65]

February 23, 1998. "Jihad Against Jews and Crusaders"[66]

"Praise be to Allah, who revealed the Book, controls the clouds, defeats factionalism, and says in His Book: "But when the forbidden months are past, then fight and slay the pagans wherever ye find them, seize them, beleaguer them, and lie in wait for them in every stratagem"; and peace be upon our Prophet, Muhammad Bin-'Abdallah, who said: I have been sent with the sword between my hands to ensure that no one but Allah is worshipped, Allah who put my livelihood under the shadow of my spear and who inflicts humiliation and scorn on those who disobey my orders.

The Arabian Peninsula has never -- since Allah made it flat, created its desert, and encircled it with seas -- been stormed by any forces like the crusader armies spreading in it like locusts, eating its riches and wiping out its plantations. All this is happening at a time in which nations are attacking Muslims like people fighting over a plate of food. In the light of the grave situation and the lack of support, we and you are obliged to discuss current events, and we should all agree on how to settle the matter.

No one argues today about three facts that are known to everyone; we will list them, in order to remind everyone:

First, for over seven years the United States has been occupying the lands of Islam in the holiest of places, the Arabian Peninsula, plundering its riches, dictating to its rulers, humiliating its people, terrorizing its neighbors, and turning its bases in the Peninsula into a spearhead through which to fight the neighboring Muslim peoples.

If some people have in the past argued about the fact of the occupation, all the people of the Peninsula have now acknowledged it. The best proof of this is the Americans' continuing aggression against the Iraqi people using the Peninsula as a staging post, even though all its rulers are against their territories being used to that end, but they are helpless.

Second, despite the great devastation inflicted on the Iraqi people by the crusader-Zionist alliance, and despite the huge number of those killed, which has exceeded 1 million... despite all this, the Americans are once against trying to repeat the horrific massacres, as though they are not content with the protracted blockade imposed after the ferocious war or the fragmentation and devastation.

So here they come to annihilate what is left of this people and to humiliate their Muslim neighbors.

Third, if the Americans' aims behind these wars are religious and economic, the aim is also to serve the Jews' petty state and divert attention from its occupation of Jerusalem and murder of Muslims there. The best proof of this is their eagerness to destroy Iraq, the strongest neighboring Arab state, and their endeavor to fragment all the states of the region such as Iraq, Saudi Arabia, Egypt, and Sudan into paper statelets and through their disunion and weakness to guarantee Israel's survival and the continuation of the brutal crusade occupation of the Peninsula.

All these crimes and sins committed by the Americans are a clear declaration of war on Allah, his messenger, and Muslims. And ulema have throughout Islamic history unanimously agreed that the jihad is an individual duty if the enemy destroys the Muslim countries. This was revealed by Imam Bin-Qadamah in "Al- Mughni," Imam al-Kisa'i in "Al-Bada'i," al-Qurtubi in his interpretation, and the shaykh of al-Islam in his books, where he said: "As for the fighting to repulse, it is aimed at defending sanctity and religion, and it is a duty as agreed. Nothing is more sacred than belief except repulsing an enemy who is attacking religion and life."

On that basis, and in compliance with Allah's order, we issue the following fatwa to all Muslims:

The ruling to kill the Americans and their allies -- civilians and military -- is an individual duty for every Muslim who can do it in any country in which it is possible to do it, in order to liberate the al-Aqsa Mosque and the holy mosque from their grip, and in order for their armies to move out of all the lands of Islam, defeated and unable to threaten any Muslim. This is in accordance with the words of Almighty Allah, "and fight the pagans all together as they fight you all together," and "fight them until there is no more tumult or oppression, and there prevail justice and faith in Allah."

This is in addition to the words of Almighty Allah: "And why should ye not fight in the cause of Allah and of those who, being weak, are ill-treated? -- women and children, whose cry is: 'Our Lord, rescue us from this town, whose people are oppressors; and raise for us from thee one who will help!'"

We -- with Allah's help -- call on every Muslim who believes in Allah and wishes to be rewarded to comply with Allah's order to kill the Americans and plunder their money wherever and whenever they find it. We also call on Muslim ulema, leaders, youths, and soldiers to launch the raid on Satan's U.S. troops and the devil's supporters allying with them, and to displace those who are behind them so that they may learn a lesson.

Almighty Allah said: "O ye who believe, give your response to Allah and His Apostle, when He calleth you to that which will give you life. And know that Allah cometh between a man and his heart, and that it is He to whom ye shall all be gathered."

Almighty Allah also says: "O ye who believe, what is the matter with you, that when ye are asked to go forth in the cause of Allah, ye cling so heavily to the earth! Do ye prefer the life of this world to the hereafter? But little is the comfort of this life, as compared with the hereafter. Unless ye go forth, He will punish you with a grievous penalty, and put others in your place; but Him ye would not harm in the least. For Allah hath power over all things."

Almighty Allah also says: "So lose no heart, nor fall into despair. For ye must gain mastery if ye are true in faith.""

Usama bin Laden's 1995 Open Letter to King Fahd focused on one overarching message, which demanded the King abdicate his throne and remove his cabinet from office much as King Saud once abdicated. This message was supported by a series of supporting points centered on Usama bin Laden's assumption that:

1. King Fahd was corrupt;
2. King Fahd squandered the Nation's wealth;
3. King Fahd was, himself, an Infidel since he supported the Jews and Crusaders; and
4. The Nation was not prepared to defend itself despite large investments in military hardware.

July 11, 1995. "An Open Letter to King Fahd On the Occasion of the Recent Cabinet Reshuffle."[67]

"Grace be to God, and prayer and peace upon the Messenger of God, his companions, and all those who followed his righteous path.

To the king of Najd and Hijaz Fahd bin 'Abd-al-Aziz. Peace be upon he who followed the righteous path. We send to you this open letter void of royal formalities and majestic titles. It is a guileless approach to you with some remarks about the atrocities you and your clan have perpetrated against God and His religion, against the rights of His worshipers and His country, and against the sanctity of His holy lands and nation. Because of the clarity of the truth we are expressing here and the elucidation of the precise contents of this letter compels us to hope that you will break the blinders that you have surrounded yourself with, thus blocking you from listening to the truth in addition to the walls that keep it from reaching your ears.

O King! The reason for writing this letter is what you and the influential executive princes do by deceiving people and your efforts to play on their minds and the transference of their wrath upon you and their resentment of your rule. Also, what you perform of …marginal and deceptive reforms that may be categorized as temporal tranquilizers for people's ire and transient pacifiers for its bitterness. This was clear when you established the Advisory Council which the nation has long awaited for. Unfortunately, the people were disappointed as it turned out that the Council was stillborn. Furthermore, your marginal cabinet reshuffle did not really cure the cause of the disease and the root of the affliction which is you, your ministers of defense and interior, the Emir of Riyadh, and all those of their ilk.

The opportunity for writing this important letter will not drive us away from the essence of our differences with you and the root of the conflict with your reign. This essence and this root are not what might rush to your mind as to what rumors you have spread during your reign and empowered your successor to oppress the simple people and deprive them of their rights especially the scholars, missionary workers, reformists, merchants, and tribal elders. It is neither what you exposed the nation, in general, to insulting its dignity and honor, sacrileged its holy lands, plundered its resources, and robbed its wealth nor what is prevalent during your reign of bribes and commissions which led to the spread of favoritism, moral and administrative corruption. Nor it is how you have led the country to the edge of an astounding economic collapse that consequently led it to the brink of bankruptcy. We shall touch on some of these important issues later on after we first present the essence and the root of our differences with you. These differences are manifested in your regime while not adhering to the principles of 'There is no God but Allah' and all that follows it. These are the foundations of monotheism which distinguish between infidelity and faith. Because all these matters result from your regime not adhering to the principles of monotheism and its necessities and since we shall soon issue –God willing- a research that would handle the aspects of this departure in more detail, we will limit our brief letter to explain two facets of this departure. They are:

First: Your Ruling with other than what God has revealed and legalizing It

The frequency of the texts of Koran, the Sunna, and the statements of the nation's scholars tell us that whoever permits himself or others to follow a positive or man-made law is transgressing God's Law and therefore is an infidel and an apostate who no longer belongs to our religious community...God, the glorified and the Almighty says,

"Hast thou not turned thy vision to those who declare that they believe in the revelations that have come to thee and to those before thee? Their real wish is to resort together for judgment to the Evil One, though they were ordered to reject him. But Satan's wish is to lead them astray far away.

Sura 9:60

Shaykh 'Abd-al-Rahman bin Hasan Al Shaykh … May God rest his soul in peace, says in interpreting this verse: Whoever seeks an arbitrator other than God and His messenger has abandoned what Muhammad, may God pray upon him and grant him salvation, had revealed and desired other than he, and made a partner for God in obedience and disagreed with what the messenger, may God pray upon him and grant him salvation, had revealed regarding what God the Almighty says: "And this: Judge thou between them by what Allah hath revealed, and follow not their vain desires, but beware of them lest they beguile thee from any of that which Allah hath sent down to thee."

Sura 5:49

Also, God the glorified says:

" But no, by the Lord, they can have no Faith until they make thee judge in all disputes between them, and find in their souls no resistance against Thy decisions, but accept them with the fullest conviction."

Sura 9:65

Whoever disobeys what God and His messenger, May God pray upon him and grant him salvation, have ordained by passing judgment among the people by anything but what God had revealed or demanded that following his desires and wishes has thus repudiated the noose of Islam and the faith. If he alleges he is a believer, then God, the glorified, has denounced whoever wanted that and disclosed his lying in alleging faith for what is contained in God's statement 'declare' thus negating their faith. If they allege, it is frequently said for the one who claims legal proceedings in which he is lying for his violating His Word and committing what negates it.

This proves God's verse: "though they were ordered to reject him." because to blaspheme against the Evil One is the cornerstone of monotheism as mentioned in the al-Baqarah verse. If this cornerstone is absent, it is not monotheistic. Monotheism is the foundation of faith with which all acts are refined and are spoiled without...as is evident in God Almighty statement. "Whoever rejects Evil and believes in Allah hath grasped the most trustworthy handhold." To arbitrate to the Evil One is to believe in him.

Shaykh Muhammad bin Ibrahim Al al-Shaykh, May God rest his soul in peace, says in interpreting this verse, " God has negated faith to anyone who wanted to arbitrate contrary to what the messenger of God, may God pray upon him and grant him salvation, revealed of the hypocrites as God Almighty says: "Hast thou not turned thy vision to those who declare that they believe in the revelations that have come to thee and to those before thee? Their real wish is to resort together for judgment to the Evil One, though they were ordered to reject him. But Satan's wish is to lead them astray far away.

Sura 9:60

When God says 'declare' that is a denial of what they have alleged of faith. Arbitration contrary to what the prophet, May God pray upon him and grant him salvation, has taught cannot be united by any means in the heart of a worshiper because each negates the other.

The words 'Evil One' are derived from tyranny which is exceeding the limit. Anyone who arbitrates differently from what the prophet, may God pray upon him and grant him salvation, revealed or judged contrary to what the prophet, may God pray upon him and grant him salvation, revealed, he then has ruled with the Evil One and accepted the rule of the tyrant and is run by the his rules.

A.H. [From the letter of Shaykh Muhammad bin Ibrahim Al al-Shaykh called. Applying the Laws.

God the Almighty says, "Do they then seek after a judgment of Ignorance? But who, for a people whose faith is assured, can give better judgment than Allah?"

Sura 5:50

Says Ibn Kathir in interpreting this verse," God denies upon everyone who digresses from His solid rule that encompasses all that which is good, prohibits all that which is evil, and rectified those opinions and vain desires and the conventions created by men without any reliance or reasoning to God's law just like the people before Islam were ruling with delusions and ignorance which they set forth with their opinions and capriciousness. Similarly, as the Tartars ruled based on the royal policies taken from their King Genkhis Khan who established for them the *al-Yasiq*, which is a medley of laws Genkhis Khan derived from Judaism, Christianity, Islam, and others. The al-Yasiq contains many rules set forth by his whims and thus they became a jurisdiction followed and preferred over judgment by Allah's Book and the Sunna of His messenger, may God pray upon him and grant him salvation. He who follows that is an infidel who must be fought until the rule of God and His messenger is regained so that no one else judges no more no less. Is this al-Yasiq a progressive example for the positive laws that you, your regime, and those of the ilk rule by today?

The arbitration of the positive laws and ruling by them is doubtlessly the worshipping of those who do that to the maker of these laws and is enslavement by the lawmaker to those who follow and obey him in all his legislations without the need for God. This meaning has been illustrated by the messenger of God, may God pray upon him and grant him salvation, to 'Uday bin Hatam in a Hadith that was reported by al-Tarmadhi and others, and which he improved. It said that 'Uday bin Hatam, may God be pleased with him, – who was a Christian- heard the prophet, may God pray upon him and grant him salvation, reading this verse, " They take their priests and their anchorites to be their lords in derogation of Allah, and Christ, the son of Mary."

Sura 9:31

He told the messenger of God that," We do not worship them!"

He said, may God pray upon him and grant him salvation, "Do not they prohibit what God has permitted and then you prohibit it? Do not they allow what He prohibited and then you allow it?" He said yes. Said the prophet,"That's what they worship."

'Uday bin Hatam, may God be pleased with him, thought that worshiping was merely limited to offering religious rites such as prayers and the like. Since the Christians do not pray for their priests and monks, he thought the Christians did not take them as their lords. But the messenger of God, may God pray upon him and grant him salvation, removed this confusion from him and made it clear for him that by obeying them in prohibiting and permitting goes contrary to God's Revelation. They have made them lords unto themselves in derogation of God. This meaning of worship...which the messenger, may God pray upon him and grant him salvation, made clear to 'Uday bin Hatam, may God be pleased with him, is the one that the nation unanimously agreed upon and was a recurrent theme among the scholarly leaders whose sayings we shall briefly mention next: Ibn Hazm reports of what God says, "They take their priests and their anchorites to be their lords in derogation of Allah,": "Since Jews and Christians prohibit what their priests and anchorites prohibited and allow what they permitted, then it is true lordship and true worship they have professed. God the Almighty called this work taking lords in derogation of Allah and worship. This is, undisputedly, polytheism in derogation of God."

Ibn Taymiyyah, a shaykh of Islam, may God rest his soul in peace, said after he mentioned the abovementioned tale of 'Uday bin Hatam: "And so said Abu-al-Bukhtari: They did not pray for them had they ordered them to worship them in derogation of God, they would not obey them. However, they ordered them and they allowed the forbidden and made the forbidden permissible. And they obeyed them. That was lordship...The prophet, may God pray upon him and grant him salvation, made it clear that their worship of the priests and anchorites was in allowing the forbidden and making the forbidden permissible. It is not that they prayed for them, fasted for them and called upon them in derogation of God but it is the worship of men. And…God has mentioned that such worship is polytheism when He says, "There is no God but He, praise and glory to Him: from having the partners they associate." Shaykh Muhammad bin 'Abd-al-Wahab, may God rest his soul in peace, classifying the abovementioned tale of 'Uday bin Hatam, "He who obeys the scholars and the princes in disallowing what God has permitted and allowing what He has rendered impermissible, has made them unto lords. The Shaykh of Islam, Ibn Taymiyyah says, may God rest his soul in peace, says," By necessity, it is known about the religion of Islam and the unanimity of all Muslims that whosoever allows himself to profess a religion other that of Islam and to follow the Shari'ah other than that of Muhammad's, may God pray upon him and grant him salvation, is an infidel." A.H. Ibn Taymiyyah, may God rest his soul in peace, continues to say, "Islam comprises submission to God alone. Therefore, he who submits to Allah and to others is an idolater. He who does not submit to Him is regarded haughty in his worship and the idolater and the haughty who do not worship him are both infidels. Submission to God alone comprises His worship alone and obedience to none other but He." The former Mufti of the Kingdom, Shaykh Muhammad bin Ibrahim al Al-Shaykh, may God rest his soul in peace, says, "The gravest manifest blasphemy is the revelation of the cursed law…the status of the honest spirit that revealed to the heart of Muhammad, may God pray upon him and grant him salvation, to become a messenger of warnings in pure and clear Arabic language to govern the universe and refer to the Book whenever people are in dispute.

In a letter addressed to the Emir of Riyadh at that time in regards to the positive laws which he referred to in the commerce chamber in

Riyadh that show that it is blasphemy out of the religious community "Consider some of the laws to pass judgment by at the least doubtlessly he was dissatisfied with the judgment of God and His messenger, the ratio of the judgment of God and His messenger to are considered insufficient or lacking. They do not perform well enough in solving the dispute bringing the rights to their lords, rule of laws to perfection, people's contentment in solving their own problems, and believing this is blasphemy and apostasy. The issue is extremely important and it is not one of the independent theological judgments."

"To arbitrate with God's law alone above every other is the closest to worshiping the Lord alone above any one else. The content of the two testaments is that God is the one worshipped alone without any partners and that His messenger is the one to be followed with what he revealed only. Swords of jihad were drawn from their sheaths for the sole purpose of defending Islam and resorting to the Revelation when controversy arises."

Scholar Shaykh Muhammad Al-Amin al-Shanqiti says in his book 'Lights of the Quran 'Judging the regime that rules contrary to the laws of the Creator of the heavens and earth in the souls of the society, their wealth, their honor, their lineage is considered blasphemy against the Creator of heavens and earth and has rebelled against the heavenly system which He placed in motion by creating all the creatures. He the Almighty God knows about their welfare more than anyone and there cannot be another legislator with Him of a higher status, "What! Have they partners who have established for them some religion without the permission of Allah." "Say, see you what things Allah hath sent down to you for sustenance? Let you hold forbidden somethings thereof and lawful. Say, hath Allah indeed permitted you, or do ye invent to attribute to Allah."

In his comments on the Book of Monotheism, Shaykh Muhammad Hamid al-Fiqqi, May God rest his soul in peace, says in regards to legislator of the positive laws the he is doubtlessly a renegade infidel if he insists on them and does not refer to what God has revealed. Whatever name he calls himself is with no avail nor will any good deed such as prayer, fasting, the Hajj, and such help him."

Shaykh Ahmad Muhammad Shakir, May God rest his soul in peace, says in regards to the arbitration of the positive laws, "This action is the shunning of God's law and a desire to move away from…His religion and a preference of the positive laws of the infidels over God's, the Almighty, laws. This is a blasphemy none of the people of the Kiblah differ regarding the accusation of infidelity of the person who says or advocates it. These are true evidences from the revelation and excerpts from scholars candid enough to replace conflict, cut off differences, silence controversy and deafen arrogance. Lest it should get too wordy, we shall not continue further with more of these proofs and excerpts. This issue constitutes a major topic in the entire Holy Quran. However, we believe what we presented is sufficient for someone who has a heart or paid attention and is a martyr.

For the remainder of the letter, we shall remind you of the practices you and your regime are following in arbitrating these blasphemous laws and voiding the rightful laws of God. An ordinary individual- let alone a scrutinizing researcher- will have no difficulty in proving that you as well as your regime are legislators and arbitrators of the positive laws, obligating people to abide by their rulings. A quick look at the charts of commercial courts and the laws that allow and authorize bank usurious transactions and others, labor and laborers laws, the law of the Saudi Arabian army, and other godless laws which…exemplify to what extent and influence have these arbitrating and blasphemous laws achieved in this country.

The advice memorandum mentioned the existence of tens of legal boards that judge the people by the positive laws with which you govern the nation and its worshipers not to mention what runs the country in its foreign relations from those laws of which we give an example of your commitment to arbitrate to a disputes settlement board with the Assembly for Cooperation among the Gulf Nations. This board to which the disputing states, members of the council headed by the host nation Saudi Arabia, resort for arbitration is, without a doubt, a blasphemous, man-made legalistic board. Article nine of its basic system of regulations as stated in the sources of its regulations and laws begins in this manner:

The board issues its recommendations and formal legal opinions according to:

1. Rules of the system of regulation of the cooperation assembly
2. The international law
3. The international conventions
4. "Principles of the Islamic Law provided that it submits its reports concerning the issues being dealt with to the supreme council to take...any measure that it sees fit."

How mocking this is to the religion of God! And how contemptuous to His Laws!

Isn't it enough infidelity and delusion that you placed God's heavenly laws and His Quranic rulings at the bottom of the list for the sources of your rules and laws preferring the concepts of the dregs of humanity, the customs, the conventions of ignorant nations, and the rules of the unbelievers so that they become under the mercy of your supreme council to make decisions according to its whims.!

O Servant of the two great mosques!!* What would the patrons of religion, the guardians of the creed, and the callers of monotheism say when resorting to such boards, councils, and courts for arbitration!?

The answer is as clear as sunlight at noon. It rejects all kinds of hesitation, delay, stuttering, sycophancy, prevarications, or trickery as we have indicated earlier. It is flagrant infidelity and an act of apostasy as proven by the Book, the Sunna, and the unanimity of the Umma.

The following are some of formal legal opinions of distinguished scholars that clearly explain the existence of these laws on one hand and its jurisprudent ruling on the other.

Shaykh Muhammad bin Ibrahim, may God rest his soul in peace, talks about the laws of commercial courts in a message sent to the Emir of Riyadh at the time. We have laid our hands on the letter entitled 'The System of Commercial Courts in the Kingdom of Saudi Arabia. Recently, we have studied the first half of the letter and we have found that its system of positive laws to be non-Islamic. The laws that the institutions rule by reflect, in the least, and without any doubt, dissatisfaction with God's laws and those of His messenger that is thought of as being out of religion by our religious people. In another letter to the Chief Justice of the Supreme Court in Riyadh regarding the law of which is run by the Bureau of Labor and Laborers and the duties of the legal courts towards it, Shaykh Muhammad bin Ibrahim, may God rest his soul in peace, says:

"From Muhammad bin Ibrahim to the Honorable Chief Justice of the Supreme Court in Riyadh. Peace be upon you and God's blessings and mercy. So far, we have studied your speech concerning the transactions that are sent by the Bureau of Labor and Laborers which must be applied in times such as this if it were submitted to the court for debate and termination. The court has to review it because it is the heart of its work.

If the transaction was submitted to carry out a directive from the Bureau of Labor and then returned to the Chief Justice to complete it according to instructions and regulations that God has given it authority, the court is not permitted to heed such directive. Such action would be deemed not only as approval on the part of the court but also as assisting in arbitrating with laws other than what God has revealed."

On the same topic the distinguished scholar 'Abdallah bin Hamid, the chief Justice, May God rest his soul in peace, wrote in his known letter explaining that arbitration with the laws of this system is an apostate foreign to our devout people. These were some of the formal legal opinions that prove the existence of these laws on one hand and which illustrate the jurisprudent law on the other. It is needless to proceed further. The issue is plain and clear. It is a well known fact that there is a clear-cut difference between the one who commits a grave sin such as accepting interest and usury believing it is forbidden and the one who enacts laws that allow these grave sins. He who deals with usury, for example, admitting it is prohibited, is committing a sin that is one of the gravest of offenses. God forbid! As for the one who enacts and legislates laws that permit usury is a renegade infidel. It is needless to alert people's attention to the towers of usurious banks that compete in height with the minarets of the two great mosques and apply your positive laws.

God the Glorified and Almighty says, " But no, by the Lord, they can have no Faith until they make thee judge in all disputes between them, and find in their souls no resistance against Thy decisions, but accept them with the fullest conviction."

Sura 4:65

God Almighty has ruled to negate this judgment by various tools of assurances foremost among others is to swear by His Name, God the Glorified and Almighty. Then, the above verse together with what the prophet, May God pray upon him and grant him salvation, explained to Uday bin Hatam in the verse: " They take their priests and their anchorites to be their lords in derogation of Allah." invalidates any doubt a transgressor may have and cuts off all his hopes.

The Second Phase: Allegiance to the Infidels and Hostility towards Muslims

There is no attribute of the foreign policy of your regime that is more prominent than tying it to the interests of western nations, the Crusaders, and the dictatorial regimes of the Islamic countries. To prove this truth does not require a lot of effort. The distant one is acquainted with this connection before the one at hand. Your regime, which proudly brags about being the custodian of the creed and the servant of the two great mosques, is the one which announced to pay $4,000,000,000 in aid to the former Soviet Union which has not yet cleansed its hands smeared with the blood of the Muslim people in Afghanistan in 1991 A.D. You regime, the guardian of the magnanimous religion, is the one that funneled thousands of millions of dollars to the Syrian Nasiri* regime in 1982 A.D. as a reward to the slaughter of tens of thousands of Muslims in the city of Hama. It is the same rule that supported the Christian Maronites from the Lebanese Militia Party against the Muslims there. Your 'orthodox!' regime was the one that paid billions of dollars to the evil regime that was crushing Islam and Muslims in Algiers. It is your same rule which supported the Christian rebels in Southern Sudan with money and arms.

With all these terrible misfortunes and the crimes perpetrated against the people and the Nation, your regime was actually able, to a certain extent, in deceiving some of the people and deluding it about these facts. However, God refused to let the truth about you to remain undisclosed. Hence, the recent events in Yemen that ripped the final mask with which you feigned to the people and led them astray. Your political and military support for the Yemeni Communists turned to be the mortal blow that broke your political backbone and the razor that shaved away your creditability on the Islamic front. The events in Yemen trapped you in a dilemma. It showed that your support for the Afghani mujahiddin was not for the sake of Islam but for the protection of western interests that were threatened by any Soviet gains in the battles there. Otherwise, the Afghani Communist Party is no different than its counterpart in Yemen. Likewise, the Yemeni Muslim is just the same as the Afghani Muslim. The dilemma is: How do you explain your support for Muslims against the communists in Afghanistan while championing the cause of the communists in Yemen against the Muslims?

This contradiction becomes incomprehensible to those who are not aware that your policies are dictated to you from abroad by the Christian western nations with whose interests you have associated your fate. Therefore, the actual motive for your occasional support of some of the Islamic causes is not- as we explained earlier- for the love of the Islamic causes and patronage of their peoples but for the protection of the interests of the infidel western countries which may coincide with Islamic causes such as happened in Afghanistan. As evidence, you stood against the Islamic causes that go counter to western interests. You supported those interests at the expense of the causes of the Muslim people. For example, you supported the American interests against those of the Somali Muslim people. You squandered the nation's usurped funds and its coerced people. Long before that crisis and long after it, you have blessed the efforts of normalization, submission, and deception of the Palestinian cause, the mother of all Islamic causes. You continued the process of the imposed peace and submission in Palestine. You volunteered to pay a huge bulk of the cost of the process despite the economic hardship that Saudi Arabia experiences. You donated $100 million to Yasir 'Arafat's secular authority which was brought in to exercise oppressive ways against the Palestinian people that the Jewish occupation authority has so far failed to accomplish. You are at war with the Palestinian people's jihadi movements especially the Islamic Resistance Movement. All that did not prevent you from supporting 'Arafat's authority and welcomed him in Riyadh despite his hostile stance towards you during the Gulf War and his apparent support of Saddam Hussein. You accepted without opposition that insult for the sake of the American cowboy who shepherds the alleged peace process. It is no wonder that even if you were not personally satisfied with the so-called peace process, all you have to do is to condescend in response to the orders of your American guardian. Was it not the American President Clinton on a visit to the country who refused to visit you in Riyadh? Did not he insist that you submissively and humiliatingly go to meet him in the American bases in Hafar-al-Batin? With that kind of behavior, the American president wanted to prove two points: First, to emphasize that the nature of his visit was basically to inspect his forces stationed in those bases. Second: to teach you a lesson in abjectness and scorn so that you are aware that he is your true guardian even in your alleged kingdom which, in reality, is nothing else but an American protectorate governed by the American Constitution.

There is neither a doubt nor any controversy among the scholars that having infidels as allies and supporting them against Muslims is definitely inconsistent to the teachings of Islam. It was mentioned by the Shaykh of Islam Ibn Taymiyyah and Shaykh Muhammad bin 'Abd-al-Wahab as one of ten contradictions of Islam. God the Almighty Glorifies says:

"O ye who believe! Take not the Jews and the Christians for your allies and protectors; they are but allies and protectors to each other. And he amongst you that turns to them is of them. Verily Allah guideth not a people unjust." Sura 5:51

God says: "Thou wilt not find any people who believe in Allah... and the Last Day, loving those who resist Allah and His messenger, even though they were their fathers or sons, or their brothers, or their kindreds."

Sura 58:22

God the Almighty has made taking the infidels as allies and protectors without the believers as a desire for honor and glory on their part, a characteristic of the hypocrites. God says: "To the Hypocrites give the glad tidings that there is for them a grievous penalty—yea, for those who take allies unbelievers rather than believers: Is it honor they seek among them? Nay-- All honor is with Allah."

Sura 4:138-139

To have infidels as allies and protectors, as scholarly people have demonstrated, is to honor and praise them, support and cooperate with them against the believers. Besides, it means to associate with them and being guiltless on the surface. This would be apostasy if committed by anyone; he must be tried like a renegade as shown by the Book, the Sunna, and nation's scholars who are a model for us. This is capably demonstrated in this poem:

Those who take the infidels as allies and protectors are doubtlessly subjected to rejection by people of intellect. Any admirer, collaborator or supporter who publicly shows willingness to collaborate, is without a doubt a partner to them in godlessness and someone who knows not the difference between he truth and falseness. O King, what would the people of the pure creed and unadulterated monotheism say regarding your godless actions? With what would those who defend you falsely argue? God says:

"Ah! These are the sort of men on whose behalf ye may contend in this world; but who will contend will Allah on their behalf on the Day of Judgment, or who will carry their affairs through?"

Sura 4:109

Now that it has been made clear that your government has deviated from the principles of Monotheism and its true and tolerant religion of which you always boast claiming to be its protector, let's evaluate your accomplishments very subjectively in the worldly field after we have thus far unmasked your true identity by the scale of jurisdiction.

We shall discuss that with you in the following

First: The Economic Situation:

You are certainly aware that our nation sits on an oil lake that constitutes one fourth of the world's reserve of this raw material whose importance cannot be ignored. You also realize that the country produces one third of OPEC output. You know as well as we do that the daily medium national product during the recent years reached $100 million daily from oil revenues in addition to the monetary reserves estimated at $140 billion at the time you ascended to the throne. That is, more than the reserves of the United States, Britain, and France combined at the time. Given the previous statistical data figures of the economic situation and the relatively small population, the nation was on the verge of having an economic phenomenon contrary to the sound economic perception of some people who thought that the day in which the nation's economy collapses would not come, thus making our country one of the most indebted worldwide, However, your suicidal policies have disappointed the hopes of those and many others. A decade after your ascension to the throne, all prospects turned upside down and changed everything. The nation's debt reached an all-time high- 80% of its total income. The status of the citizen was transformed from the one with the highest monetary reserves to that of the most indebted in the world. The collapsing economic situation has encumbered the lives of the citizens and residents alike. They have been overburdened with excise, custom, and sales taxes. The rates of utilities such as water, electricity, in addition to food prices have skyrocketed in an unprecedented manner. The catastrophe did not leave the status of education untouched. Most schools now suffer from over crowdedness in classrooms causing a lot of inconveniences to the students, teachers, and parents. What made a bad situation worse was the failure of the ministry to maintain the current classes let alone its inability to build new units. The plight of the nation's hospitals was not any better than the schools'. The government failed to provide proper maintenance for the hospitals whose many pavilions have regrettably transformed into human slaughterhouses where medicines, medical care and treatment required are lacking let alone the inability of the ministry to have new hospitals built. Even worse is the growing number of the unemployed among the ranks of the youth and the new graduates having high university degrees. The number of the unemployed who have grown worn out from trying to find an employment opportunity has risen to one hundred fifty thousands. This number increases every year resulting in a recession and the shrinkage of the labor market before their eyes because of the current economic crisis that is growing worse and worse. As this crisis intensifies and the situation gets worse, you and your government unabashedly call to the people to conserve energy consumption and other items while your attitude was the worst example for the citizens encouraging them to be more wasteful and live more luxuriously. How dare you call upon the people to conserve energy when everybody sees how your magnificent palaces are illuminated and air-conditioned all day and all night? How would anyone consent to your call to conserve spending and become austere while they see how your palaces and houses have sprawled all over the land and hears about your accounts fattened with the nation's wealth both locally and internationally?

The volume of your spending the people's wealth on those palaces and houses inside and outside the country is an astounding and scary one. It is estimated to be thousands of millions of dollars. Talking about all that would take a long time. The narrator would not know where to start. Should he start from the City of Jedda and the artificial magnificent isles on which you have erected the most splendid palaces on the largest areas of the coast? Or should the narrator begin with Riyadh where building palaces on the earth surface was not sufficient so you had to build underneath? Or should he start with your mansions in Muna, Ta'if, al-Huda, al-Shafa, Mecca, Medina and all other towns of the Kingdom? Or should he ignore all this and begin with the palaces in the other western capitals and resorts? Those mansions most of which you have not stepped into and most probably will not visit them for the remainder of your life. If these statements came from other sources, you would be able to deny but you know very well who is addressing you and that they are the most knowledgeable about these facts that are no longer beyond the reach of the public let alone the private. "And none, Can tell thee like the One Who is acquainted with all things."

Sura 35:14

You and those among your elite circle have a passion for building palaces and amassing treasures. Competing among you for those ardent desires was a major reason behind directing most of your efforts and time towards achieving that goal. Competition has torn your relationships asunder after arousing the resentment and wrath of some of you which led to the monopolization of material privileges by you and those closest to you. What Muhammad, May God pray upon him and grant him salvation, said on one occasion applies to this situation: "Miserable are those who worship money and fine clothes. They are happy when they are provided and upset when they are denied." This wastefulness and spending of the nation's wealth, your concern for personal interests, and competing among yourselves about all that were among the most prominent reasons that led the country into the bankruptcy pit. This is where your 'orthodox' policies have led us. "Verily spendthrifts are brothers of the Evil Ones."

Sura 17:27

The current economic crisis and whatever risks it warns us of, and what impact it would have were not without precedents and causes. It was the outcome of a number of fatal actions and policies that you and the executives of your ruling clan have committed. Some of the most significant of these causes in addition to what we have alluded to such as spendthrift and wastefulness that you practice are:

1. Your Role in the Decline in Oil Prices:

Since the eighties, oil prices have been plummeting. However, the impact of this sudden price decline on the nation's economy was not felt publicly until the nineties when you always resorted to the nation's reserve fund to cover the continued budget deficit. The unwise policies have run the nation's reserve funds dry and failed to offer any solution to the crisis that is growing aggravatingly on a daily basis. As a reminder, you very well know that the absolute subordination you have demonstrated to the policies of the western nations and their directives to you to support your former friend Saddam Hussein with $25 billion and to increase oil production in order to lower the prices to harm Iran during the war with Saddam had an enormous role in the sudden decline of oil prices to their current level which basically serves the interests of the western consumers. Despite the fact that the West is careful enough not to slaughter the Saudi chicken that lays black gold for them, they are extremely cautious that the price tag on this egg remains at a minimum.

2. Lack of serious action to find other sources for income:

It is well known that oil as a source of revenue is bound to be depleted and prices always tend to fluctuate. Although the nation is well prepared to develop other sources for income which are available and in abundance, however, your regime has failed to expand those resources and the country continues to depend almost entirely on oil revenues.

3. Out of control spending at the expense of coalition forces during the Gulf War:

Even though our nation was suffering from financial hardship during the Gulf War and despite the fact that the objective of the western countries was nothing but the annihilation of the Iraqi army and the Muslim people of Iraq before anything else, they seized on any available opportunity... to rob you of your money and exploit your fear and cowardice. Thus, you ended up paying the war bill almost in its entirety having spent $60 billion for that purpose. Half of this bill was pocketed by the Americans and about $15 billion went to the rest of the allies. The remainder was spent on transactions, deals, and local bribes. Not only did the war cost stop at this point but also you pledged your allegiance to the allied countries by striking other deals as a reward for them in the post-war period. An inconceivable price of $40 billion was paid for the Americans only just to cover the cost of military and civilian deals. Besides, as a courtesy to the British Prime Minister, John Major, you struck a deal to purchase the British Tornado jet planes even though our nation's army lacked the human expertise to fly them as was proven during the Gulf War. What is even worse, those airplanes were found unsuitable as witnessed by the army technical commission. We shall discuss this issue in more detail later on. And instead of initiating a useful policy to avoid the situation and handle the collapsed economy, you and your regime took some suicidal economic measures that made things even worse. These policies include:

1. The exhaustion of the nation's financial assets abroad:

Earlier, we mentioned that the nation's available assets were estimated at $140 billion when you first ascended to the throne. The Kingdom's annual income for that period was estimated at $97 billion. Think with us for a moment and imagine how your spending spree totally and ridiculously squandered those assets a mere seven years after your ascension to the throne.

2. Interest loans from local and international banks:

Despite the fact that there are a lot of fervent warnings regarding the handling of interest and usury and even though there are those who launch war against God's principles, "If ye do it not, take notice of war from Allah and His messenger," and despite what reality has proven about the system of interest loans introduced by banks which make the poor even poorer day after day, you and your regime have drowned the nation in a sea of debts. Nothing on the horizon indicates the possibility of eliminating even the usurious interests when the nation is incapacitated and unable to simply pay off those usurious interests.

Let me give you an example of the volume of those debts. In 1411H alone, you were forced to borrow tens of billions of dollars from the local and international banks. By the year 1414H, these debts with the compounded interest rendered the state unable to keep its commitments to loan issuers. This means just paying the interest would continue to encumber the nation's budget let alone the paying off of the principal. Thus, you have left the future of the country and the future of the coming generations mortgaged in the grip of international organizations. Not only do these organizations control the economy of the indebted nations but also extend their control to the political decisions of their regimes. In addition to all this, the government owes 200 billion Riyals to more than 3000 merchants and contractors and is procrastinating to pay them off.

With that kind of management, you have broken an all-time record in squandering and extravagance of the public funds before you and have far surpassed your predecessors and succeed you. Congratulations to you for such a feat! And this is not unlike you because people of your ilk lack a vision for a better future for their country and people. What matters to them is to follow their personal lusts and selfish whims. While continuing those preposterous actions, you have forgotten the horrible fates that befell the Shah of Iran, Marcos of the Philippines, and Ceausescu of Romania and others. Those who dry out the livelihood of their people and are indifferent to their destiny will eventually meet similar tragic death. Truly, the country is experiencing the most critical economic crises that it had encountered until now. The first crisis took place during the chaotic reign of King Saud which led to his deposition in the year 1384/1385 H. The second crisis occurred in 1406 H because of the sudden dip in oil prices. If the first crisis was overcome by deposing King Saud and his entourage and the second by resorting to the enormous reserve funds of the nation at the time, then the current one does not appear to bring any happy tidings in the foreseeable future. This is because the national monetary fund has been totally squandered on one hand and the financial credibility both locally and abroad has been irreparably damaged on the other. Your failure to deal with the crisis at a time when the nation enjoyed a reserve fund estimated at $140 billion and was debt free was the most convincing evidence of your incompetent handling of the crisis after you dissipated the reserve fund and immersed the nation in an avalanche of usurious debts.

"If you cannot manage a situation when things are in your favor," a poet once said," You cannot do better when matters fly off the hands."

It is useless for your media machine to continue deluding the people and playing deceptive tricks on them by telling them that the crisis is about to end. The lies that your media apparatus is weaving and its deception will no longer pass unnoticed because the nation has reached the point of awareness saturation. These ignominious lies will no longer be credible. By squandering the nation's finances and being such a spendthrift and your lies to the people, you have merged all the attributes that God has ruled against such a person," Truly Allah guides not one who transgresses and lies!"

Sura 40:28.

This is for an ordinary person. But if the liar is the King, then the punishment is much harsher than to others as it was reported in the *Sahih Prophetic Tradition* by Muslim. On Judgment Day, three persons God neither talks to, nor absolves them, nor looks at them and their agony is painful: a fornicating old man, a lying king, and an arrogant family breadwinner.

Given all the previous indications, it appears that the solution that ended the crisis-prone King Saud's reign by having him abdicate is the most favorable one currently recommended.

Prior to that, the patched-up solutions ahead of you remain bitter and cruel on one hand, unbeneficial and ineffective on the other. Are you going to resort, for example, to devaluing the Riyal? This measure may give you a brief break. However, such step has political repercussions which would prove to be riskier than economic. Are you going to risk your ambitious prestige of aspiring to become the leader of the Cooperation

Council and devalue the Riyal in return for the other nations' currencies? Of course, your political ambition and your love for leadership will be an obstacle for that especially that leading these nations is all that is left of your broad leading dream. That entire dream was shattered because you failed to achieve any significant prestige in the Arab and Islamic world of which our nation was once boasting and leading during King Faysal's reign. Or do you want to raise the taxes and the customs on the citizens and residents to raise funds for the bankrupt treasury? This step may doubtlessly succeed in guaranteeing a measure of liquidity. Nevertheless, its political aftermath might hinder you from moving forward for a considerable period of time. The citizen, out of necessity, may choose to be silent as you squander the public wealth. However, he may act otherwise seeing all the taxes and customs being taken from his hard-won wages to be frivolously spent for the personal escapades and the dissoluteness of the wanton and the influential members of your ruling dynasty.

There is another solution before you: sell all the nation's organizations to the private sector. Even though you have taken some considerable measures in this regards, however, there are many road blocks that hinder your efforts and we appreciate that on our part. The embarrassment and the disgrace that may trail you because of selling these organizations which you consider as private family possessions and what selling them publicly tell about the level of your bankruptcy are issues that are assessed and considered by many who know your adherence to splendor, ostentation, arrogance, and pride. Your problem is that these partial solutions along with their bitterness and injustice are the better of two evils to you. This is because the fundamental solutions mean only one thing: the elimination of the causes of the crisis. Continuing to rule the country tops the list of those causes. Tragically for you, the difficult equation is your staying will be the cause of your destruction and continuation spells the end of you.

Second: The Military Situation:

You probably agree with us that the army has taken up one third of the national budget for many decades. Meanwhile, if you look at a nuclear power state like France, you will find that it spends only 4% of its budget on its army. You will not disagree with us as well that the Saudi army, despite the astronomical amounts squandered for it, is in fact but a pile of stacked weapons and equipment lacking the manpower to use. It is small wonder then to know that what was spent on the army was not spent to strengthen and train it but to provide a source of living for the influential princes and to become a fund-pumping machine for compensation to those who provide protection for your throne and your western masters with whom you have signed many deals as a tax for being humiliated and subordinated. For example, the purchase of seventy F15 jet fighters from America was only meant to consolidate George Bush's base in his reelection campaign after the Gulf War. Likewise, the deals for the Saudi Airlines fleet and the expansion of telephone communications system were only intended to please Clinton whose feelings were hurt because of your support of his opponent George Bush. For the same reasons, 48 Tornado jet fighters were purchased from Great Britain.

And if we understand the motives behind all these deals, we will realize the secret of the disgraceful performance of the Minister of Defense during the Gulf War.

Throughout the war, the Saudi Air Force with 500 jet fighters under its command was not able to perform any memorable feats except the downing of two Iraqi planes which lacked any air cover.

As for the naval force which boasts thirty battleships twenty of them with rocket launchers, the ministry failed to launch anything throughout the war. Land armor did not fare well either. To put one brigade into action, the country was forced to bring in Pakistani technical teams.

Thus, hundreds of millions of dollars that were spent on this army had gone with the wind.

One cannot help but wonder with utter amazement when one lets figures speak about the expenditures of the ministry of defense. The ministry has been run by the oldest minister in the world, Prince Sultan who appears to be asking for more time to prove his competence after the humiliating defeat that he suffered and what the events of the Gulf War have eventually revealed.

In order for us to consider the baffling picture of the expenditures of this ministry, it would be enough to know that the citizen in the Arabian Peninsula shouldered more spending for military purposes than his counterpart in ten other countries combined. These are: the United States of America, Germany, Italy, Egypt, Romania, Spain, Poland, Ecuador, Uruguay, and Ireland. In 1992, the citizen in the Peninsula has spent more than his counterpart in these ten nations combined knowing that some of these nations are nuclear powers and members of the North Atlantic Treaty Organization. Another aspect of this mind-boggling scenario becomes crystal clear if we know that one individual in the armed forces of the Arabian Peninsula cost the military more than what was spent on his counterpart in nine countries combined. These are: The United States of America, Germany, Belgium, Argentine, China, Iran, the Zionist enemy, South Korea, and Tanzania.

Then, do we not have the right to ask you O King where did all those amounts go? You don't have to answer if you knew the rate of transactions and bribes that you and the influential princes earn, headed by the minister of defense Sultan, from the arms dealers or companies and the contracts signed for the reconstruction of cities and military bases. We shall not bother much to ask about the fate of the other amounts that are spent. It is no longer a secret that you and the gangs of princes around you pocket a rate between 40-60% from the value of each deal you strike.

The greater portion of the remaining funds is spent on building bases and providing equipment and supplies whose colossal volume and high quality are not commensurate with the number and efficiency of the army. The heart of the matter is that these bases were not constructed for the Saudi army but to be used by the American and western forces already stationed in many of them. By the way, since I mentioned these forces, do not we have the right to question the objective for allowing them to remain on the land of the two Great Mosques with all their staggering numbers and equipment? Does Iraq still pose a real danger to your throne after the destruction of its army and the starvation of its Muslim people? All facts tend to prove otherwise and emphasize that the danger these forces are stationed here to deter is not an illusive peril from a starved and destroyed Iraq but, as the experts suggest, from the Islamic danger on the inside since the kingdom is witnessing a blessed and heightened Islamic awakening in all the military and civilian sectors. Be it as it may, there is no justification for leaving the nation's army to experience a state of incapacitation and negligence whereas it was supposed to safeguard the land of the Muslims and defend their causes in addition to protecting the holy lands. It is not reasonable to keep one's silence about transforming the nation to an American protectorate to be defiled by the soldiers of the Cross with their soiled feet in order to protect your crumbling throne and the preservation of the oilfields in the kingdom.

In light of the present reality, O King, is it not the right of the nation to wonder about who is behind shaking the security of the country and causing disturbance? Is it the system that delivered the country into the state of chronic military debilitation in order to justify bringing the Jewish and Christian forces to defile the holy lands? Or is it the person who calls for the preparation of the nation, arming it to be strong enough to take matters into its hands, protection of its honor and religion, defense of its holy sites, its land, and dignity?

The truth is that the blame game in this regard falls in your backyard and that of your defense minister. It excludes other individuals of the army and the guards many of whom are known to be honest, decent, and brave but unfortunately, they are not in any significant position.

You have always feared that these honest people might one day achieve some reform which would push you to marginalize many of their officers and soldiers and plant spies among them. You were afraid of any probable coordinated act among the various factions of the armed forces to carry out any reform action against you. That was the reason behind not allowing them to make any coordination or even adequate acquaintances among themselves along for the necessity of coordination for any successful military action. The price you paid for the preservation of your throne and doing away with fear illusions that continue to haunt you is what has befallen the nation and its citizens of dishonor, ignominy, destruction, and collapse because of the war in the Gulf.

Summary and Conclusions: From what we said above, it is proven, O King, that your regime has committed the forbidden things in Islam which nullify its validity before God. The devastating failure and the dishonorable corruption which have been proven against your regime are enough reasons to overthrow it. By legislating the positive blasphemous laws and obligating people to seek judgment by them, by pledging your allegiance and support to the infidels against the Muslims, you have committed many of the things which are contrary to the teachings of Islam and which demand that you be revolted against and removed.

By its devastating corruption and dishonorable failure in the areas of defense economy, and others, it was practically proven that the regime is not qualified to be at the helm of running the country's ship even if he had not violated the teachings of Islam and becoming a renegade. O King! You have combined in your character all the attributes of evil: infidelity and poverty.

Based on what we have said so far, it is evident that the nation, headed by its scholars, missionaries, reformers, merchants, and the tribal elders being at odds with your regime is neither an accidental difference nor a transient conflict. It is an embedded struggle between two methods and a profound conflict between two creeds; A conflict between the perfectly divine program which submitted the fate to God in all matters, "Say: Truly my prayer and my service of sacrifice, my life and my death, are all for Allah, the Cherisher of the Worlds; No partner hath He: This am I commanded, and I am the first of those who bow to His Will."

Sura 6: 162-163

This is the comparison between the method of 'there is no god but Allah and Muhammad is His messenger' with all its meanings, significance, and principles, and the crude secular method, the method of, "Do you opt to believe in parts of the Book and reject some other parts of it?" the method of, "Fain would they deceive Allah and those who believe, but they only believe themselves, and realize it not."

Sura 2: 9

According to what was already said above, the nation is up against your regime led by its scholars, reformers, merchants, and tribal elders. Because your regime has long lost its legitimacy as we explained earlier, removing you will decidedly not be considered in the category of the forbidden. Someone who lacks legitimacy is juristically equal to someone who has no perception as ruled by our scholars. If a ruler reneges, he has to resign as unanimously proclaimed by our nation. However, this does not mean that any conduct of this sort is necessarily the right one. Each phase of change has its own constituents, its methods, and objectives.

That cannot be specifically achieved by rash personal effort or an individual provocative decision. It has to be accomplished by the nation's leadership of honest scholars, missionaries, and reformers whose hardships and misfortunes have proven their competence and qualifications to confront such grand undertakings.

Certainly, there is no doubt that some of the things in the forefront of the present phase duties include: Coming out openly with the truth, declare it publicly, explain the meanings and principles of 'There is no god but Allah' and the consequences which are considered upon reneging them so that the nation can have an insight into its religion and be aware of its affairs.

Regardless of all this, we deem it right, O King that it is to your personal advantage the family and those around you. We ask that you abdicate. You are getting older and you are ill. You suffer from internal and external crises. By doing so, you will save the nation and the people needless trouble, hardship, crises, and disturbances. You will feel relaxed and rested letting the nation exercise its rights through the influential people and choose the ones who will rescue them from the bottomless pit you have led them into. Presently, your condition is hopeless and there is no way to turn the wheels back. You have aged too much. Long time ago, a poet said:

"The old impudent and foolish man can no longer meditate and he becomes incompetent while a lad attains maturity after being through being foolish for some time." Let me remind you here about how King Saud was forced to relinquish his throne for reasons which would pale tenfold compared to your corruption. You were in the forefront of those who sought his dethronement and you were amply applauded for your stand at the time. Today, we pray that you follow that stance not only by abdicating personally but also have all your ministers and court members who had a role in bringing the nation to this sorry state resign. It was your misdeed that set them to control the people\and their interests. Try to show a little of your good nature to relieve the people from your evil and theirs especially your disastrous defense minister who foiled any command given him whether political or administrative. He almost started a border crisis with the State of Qatar and was on the brink of a ferocious war with Yemen. In addition to all this, he failed miserably in administering the ministries of defense, Air Force, and the airlines which became bankrupt while he was its chairman.

It is extremely futile at this stage to reshuffle the cabinet with a patchwork that would bring us ministers who are subordinate to the corrupt roots of the ruling regime around which they orbit aimlessly. Even if we suppose they have good intentions and work hard to bring about reform, their marginally limited power would restrict them from any opportunity to do that because your absolute power would be hovering above them. A crooked stick cannot have a straight shadow.

These demands for abdication and dismissal of the cabinet are not crippling. They are the same demands you and your brothers sought in order to dethrone King Saud earlier.

Now, before I end my letter, we ask you to deeply contemplate and review these facts before you before you let the reins of your dignity overpower you and decide to randomly punish whoever tried to get this letter into your hands and aggravated your temperament as you have done with countless complaints and memorandums that were submitted to you. The most famous of these memorandums was the advice given to you loaded with reform acts that described the illness and prescribed the cure with the precision of a scientist, the zeal of a missionary, and the compassion of a sincere adviser in all politeness and dignity. But all you did was to ignore the counseling, disregard the advisers and even decide to punish the cream of the nation's scholars, missionaries, and reformers who submitted the memorandum to you. You sent your cavalry, all those who patronize you, their powerful committees, people of your court, and those you have misled and the collaborators to persecute them. You issued Futwas full of falsehoods and accusations of that elite group of our people and the cream of our scholars currently carrying on their lives patiently and steadfastly behind iron bars in your prison cells.

We ask God to have them released and facilitate their lives and grant us all steadfastness on the path of His Call and the means to cementing belief in His religion. "Until there is no more tumult or oppression, and there prevail justice and faith in Allah."

Sura 2: 193. We ask Him to help us to become loyal to our pledge of vengeance for His religion and avenge for His worshipers in general, those who encounter various types or torture and oppression at the hands of the executioners of your jails in particular.

Our last supplication is Praise be to the Lord of the Universe.

Usama bin Muhammad bin Laden"

Al-Qaeda Strategic Communication Blunder: Usama bin Laden Lies to the Press and Later Refutes his Statement

The following three interviews with Usama bin Laden, and amplifying statement of October 6, 2002 to Al-Jazeera, are significant from a strategic communication perspective. The Usama bin Laden and Ayman al-Zawahiri lead al-Qaeda is known for not making irrefutable strategic communication blunders. Yet in the days and months immediately following September 11th (and more importantly the intense pressure – both militarily and diplomatically) placed on al-Qaeda resulted in Usama bin Laden openly lying to the press and the world about his involvement in the September 11th attacks on the United States. Specifically, Usama bin Laden's September 28, 2001 interview with the newspaper *Ummat Karachi* and a follow-on interview with Al-Jazeera in October of 2001, show Usama bin Laden denying any interaction with the 9/11 hijackers. In mid-November, 2001 however, Usama bin Laden addressed a room of supporters in Qandahar, Afghanistan while being video taped for the world's media. The transcript and videotape were released to the world media on December 13, 2001. In this videotape Usama bin Laden states, "The brothers, who conducted the operation, all they knew was that they have a martyrdom operation and we asked each of them to go to America but they didn't know anything about the operation, not even one letter. But they were trained and we did not reveal the operation to them until they are there and just before they boarded the planes."[68] Usama bin Laden went on to say, (in response to someone in the crowd asking him to "tell the Shaykh about the dream of Abu-Da'ud") "They

97

were overjoyed when the first plane hit the building, so I said to them: be patient. The difference between the first and second plane hitting the towers was twenty minutes. And the difference between the first plane and the plane that hit the Pentagon was one hour."[69]

The interviews that follow show a stressed and very tired Usama bin Laden who in a haggard condition lies about that involvement. Several interviews later, however, he clearly takes credit for the attacks and even brags of his knowledge of building construction (and tangentially associated demolition[70]). Additionally, he makes clear his personal knowledge that more planes will strike US targets as the day progresses.

June 10, 1999 (date aired). Interview by Jamal Isma'il of Usamah Bin-Ladin in an undisclosed location within Afghanistan.[71]

"[Salah Najm] When Bin-Ladin's name is mentioned, a number of conflicting ideas cross one's mind. Wealth, asceticism, terrorist, heroism, and Jihad. What links all these words together is this man, whom some people consider to be a devil, while others believe he is a fighter with a cause.

[Usamah Bin-Ladin] Usamah Bin-Muhammad Bin-'Awad Bin-Ladin. God Almighty was gracious enough for me to be born to Muslim parents in the Arabian Peninsula, in al-Malazz neighborhood in al-Riyadh, in 1377 hegira [1957 or 1958 depending on the month in which he was born]. Then God was gracious to us as we went to Holy Medinah six months after I was born. For the rest of my life I stayed in Hejaz moving between Mecca, Jeddah, and Medinah.

As it is well known, my father, Shaykh Muhammad Bin-'Awad Bin-Ladin, was born in Hadramaut. He went to work in Hejaz at an early age, more than 70 years ago. Then God blessed him and bestowed on him an honor that no other contractor has known. He built the holy Mecca Mosque where the holy Kaabah is located and at the same time -- because of God's blessings to him -- he built the holy mosque in Medinah for our prophet, God's prayers be upon him. Then when he found out that the Government of Jordan announced a tender for restoration work on the Dome of the Rock Mosque, he gathered engineers and asked them to estimate the cost price only, without profit. They said to him: With God's help, we will be awarded the project and make some profit as well. He said to them: Calculate only the cost price of the project. When they did, they were surprised that he, God have mercy on his soul, reduced the cost price in order to guarantee that God's mosques, and this mosque in particular, are well served. He was awarded the project. Because of God's graciousness to him, sometimes he prayed in all three mosques in one single day. May God have mercy on his soul. It is not a secret that he was one of the founders of the infrastructure of the Kingdom of Saudi Arabia.

Afterward, I studied in Hejaz. I studied economy at Jeddah University, or the so-called King 'Abd-al-'Aziz University. I worked at an early age on roads in my father's company, may God have mercy on his soul. My father died when I was 10 years old.

This is something brief about Usamah Bin-Ladin. As to what he [Usamah Bin-Ladin] wants; what he wants and demands is the right of any living being. We want our land to be freed of the enemies, we want our land be free of the Americans. God equipped these living creatures with an instinctive zeal and they refuse to be intruded upon. For instance, if an armed military man walks into a chicken's home wanting to attack it, the chicken will fight back and it is only a chicken. We are demanding a right given to all living creatures, not to mention the fact that it a right for all human beings, and a right for Muslims in particular.

There was an attack on the countries of Islam, especially on the holy shrines and on al-Aqsa Mosque, the prophet's first Kiblah. And then the aggression continued with the Crusader-Jewish alliance being led by the United States and Israel. Now they have taken the country of the two holy mosques. The only source of strength is Allah.

We seek to instigate the nation to get up and liberate its land, to fight for the sake of God, and to make the Islamic law the highest law, and the word of God the highest word of all.

[S'ad-al-Din Ibrahim, journalist and social sciences professor at the American University of Cairo] With regards to Bin-Ladin, he is the exception that proves the rule, because he is the youngest child, and because his family, despite its considerable wealth, is still considered a marginal one in Saudi Arabia originating from Hadramaut, which is why he was not fully accepted in Saudi society despite his wealth. This marginalization sometimes explains the desire to rebel against the system, and if he is unable to do this on the inside, then he does it from the outside. This applies to some Saudi princes -- even in the era of [former Egyptian President Jamal] 'Abd-al-Nasir -- who were not very popular among the Saudi royal family and who rebelled against the royal family, the system, and their class as a result of attempts to marginalize them.

['Abd-al-Bari 'Atwan, editor in chief of the London-based Al-Quds al-'Arabi newspaper] I found him to be a man who is very modest in nature. He believes in every word he says. He does not lie. He does not exaggerate. He does not complement anyone. He does not even try to hide anything. He expresses everything he feels. He is very enigmatic. His voice is calm and well-mannered. I spent a whole day with him and I truly sensed his charm, his refined manners, and true modesty, not exaggerated or with fake modesty. He is a man who seeks the after-life and who truly feels that he has lived more than enough. You feel that there is a sadness inside him -- which he did not express -- that he was not martyred when he was fighting the Soviet or the communists or the heathens. You feel like he is saying: Why am I alive?

[Larry Johnson, expert on terrorism and former US intelligence officer] It is clear, he has killed and wounded more American citizens than any other group involved in terrorist attacks in the past seven years. No individual or group has killed as many Americans or foreigners. For example, if we were to count the number of victims per attack, we find that Usamah Bin-Ladin and his followers have killed about 125 victims per attack, while Hamas [Islamic Resistance Movement] -- which is number two on the list -- has killed six victims per attack.

This difference shows that Bin-Ladin is not doing the ordinary, but rather has taken it upon himself to carry out a clear mission. He believes that the United States is desecrating the cradle of Islam in Saudi Arabia, and has thus directed his war against American interests. Fortunately, his capabilities are limited; afterall he is only human. He is not a giant, he is not superman, nor can he tell the future or read minds, but he is still a threat. He has pledged to kill people and has acted on it. I think that he is a man of his word. He made a threat and we should not just consider him an idiot. We should take his threat seriously.

[Najm] Usamah Bin-Ladin is the man that the United States has declared war on, and who has declared war in return. An attempt to assassinate him has cost several hundreds of millions of dollars that fell in the form of Cruise missiles on his camp in (Khoft) mountain in Afghanistan. It is the same camp that the United States called the base. The story does not start here.

The Afghan war was just starting after a series of military coups, the first of which toppled the monarchy, and brought pro-Soviet Union governments to this hard-to-invade country. The cold war, with all its implications, hit Afghanistan: Soviet troops entered Afghanistan, the United States issued a warning:

[Former US President Jimmy Carter; archive recording of speech, date not given] I have sent a message today to the US Olympics Committee spelling out my own position, that unless the Soviets withdraw their troops within a month from Afghanistan, the Olympic games will be moved from Moscow to an alternate site or multiple sites, or postponed, or cancelled.

[Najm] The resistance movement began. The mujahidin were fighting communist atheism, while the United States was fighting the progress of Soviet influence, and for the first time in centuries, the banner of Jihad in the name of Islam and the war on the Soviets in the name of Jihad was raised. There are those who say that this holy war was launched in the name of the United States and with its support. Were the mujahidin US agents who turned against Washington when it turned on them?

[Bin-Ladin] This is a US attempt to distort things. Praise be to God who made their plots backfire on them. Every Muslim who sees discrimination begins to hate the Americans, the Jews, and Christians. This is part of our religion and faith. Since I become aware of things around me, I have been in a war, enmity, hatred against the Americans. What they claim has never happened. Saying that they supported jihad or fighting, it became clear to us that this support was from the Arab states, particularly the Gulf states, for Pakistan to encourage it to support jihad. This support was not for the sake of Almighty God, but out of fear for their thrones from the Soviet advance. At the time, Carter was the US President. He could not say anything significant until after some 20 days in 1399 [hegira], corresponding to 20 January [year not given]. He said any Russian interference in the Gulf region will be termed an aggression against the United States. This is because he occupies this region and its oil. This is why he said we will use military force if this interference takes place. The Americans are lying when they say that they cooperated with us in the past, and we challenge them to show any evidence of this. The truth of the matter is that they were a burden on us and on the mujahidin in Afghanistan. There was no agreement on this. We were doing our duty in support of Islam in Afghanistan, although this duty used to serve, against our desire, the US interests. This situation was similar to the Muslims' fight against the Romans. We know that fighting between the Romans and the Persians has always been strong. So, no wise man can say that when the Muslims fought the Romans first at the Mu'tah battle they were agents to the Persians, but interests met at this point. In other words, your killing of the Romans, which is a duty for you, used to please the Persians. However, after they finished with the Romans, they began to fight the Persians. So, the conversion of interests without agreement does not necessarily mean relations or agentry. In fact, we have been hostile to them since then. Praise be to God, we gave lectures during those days in Hejaz and Najd on the need to boycott the US goods and to attack the US forces and the US economy. This was more than 12 years ago.

[Najm] The United States has always tried to belittle the size of the role it played there, however, it admitted that it extended aid. In the US capital, Washington, Larry Johnson, a former US intelligence employee, is still doing his job of training government quarters on how to combat terrorism. He speaks about that period:

[Johnson] Several foreign powers before the Russians went into Afghanistan. The British went to Afghanistan and tried to control its people. The British and the Russians failed. I do not think that there is anyone who can control Afghanistan other than its people. However, saying that the United States went there and trained the mujahidin how to use rifles or plant explosives, this is nonsense. Did we do this? Yes, we went and helped in training and we provided them with aid which helped them in expelling the Russians. However, this was not a phenomenon that was created by the United States. This practice has been going on there for centuries, and we should realize this.

[Najm] At the beginning of that war, the Arabs used to flow into Afghanistan, mujahidin and journalists. Jamal Isma'il, al-Jazirah correspondent, used to study there at the time. He was acquainted with a wealthy young man who was full of enthusiasm of jihad against the infidels. Usamah Bin-Ladin was in Peshawar:

[Isma'il] I was first introduced to Shaykh Usamah Bin-Muhammad Bin-Ladin when he used to visit the Pakistani city of Peshawar during the Afghan jihad against the Soviet occupation of Afghanistan. At the time, I was a student at Peshawar University. I used to visit the Arab relief aid offices to report news to those interested at the time. I knew him first in 1984 when he established a services center. It was called the Mujahidin Services Center [MSC]. I knew him in the city of Peshawar in 1984 when the MSC was established in cooperation between Shaykh Usamah Bin-Muhammad Bin-Ladin and the Palestinian Shaykh 'Abdallah 'Azzam who was killed in Peshawar in 1989. At the time, Usamah Bin-Ladin used to finance the biggest part of the MSC budget and some Arab preachers or mujahidin at the Afghan fronts. However, he was not a permanent resident in Peshawar or on the Afghan territories. He used to come to these areas once every three or four months. Most of the time, he used to come to Peshawar to acquaint himself with the situation and to meet with the Afghan mujahidin leaders, Shaykh 'Abdallah 'Azzam, and others. He used to visit the internal Afghan fronts. Later, things developed for him. So, he financed the establishment of the first camp for the Arab mujahidin in 1986 or at the end of 1986. This camp began to prepare and train Arab fighters in an areas in Afghanistan and close to the Pakistani border. It was called the (Geiji).

[Golbbuddin Hekmatyar, a leading Afghan leader] Usamah Bin-Ladin came to Afghanistan when many states used to encourage their youths to go to Afghanistan to take part in the battles there. The United States also did not object to this. A number of Muslims used to come from the United States too. They participated in the battles during the Russian invasion of Afghanistan. Usamah Bin-Ladin also came at the same time. The Saudi Government also did not object to this. He stayed in Afghanistan.

[Najm] However, the losing party in this war had another viewpoint. General (Valenkov), commander of the Soviet land forces in Afghanistan, laid down his arms and became a member of the Soviet Parliament. However, several years ago, when the war was at its peak, the general was at the frontline, fighting the Mujahidin. Then he withdrew.

[Valenkov] The United States played a really decisive role. Since we sent our forces into Afghanistan, the Americans knew about our decision which was very well known. However, the Americans kept silent. They did not show any stand for fear that we might change our opinion. They wanted us to go there. But when we entered Afghanistan, they did their utmost to fully support the Afghan opposition, materially, technologically, and ideologically. They exploited the presence of Afghan refugees in Pakistan and Iran.

They provided every material need to establish military camps, training centers, arsenals, and bases. Some other countries also contributed to this, including Pakistan for a clear purpose; namely, preparing the Afghan refugees in the best possible way. Obviously, we called those who constituted armed factions gangs but they were real armed groups. They used to dispatch arms convoys to Afghanistan through Pakistan. They knew that they had definite tasks and that they were fighting not only for religion or a cause but for the substantial amounts of money they were receiving. The mujahidin had a direct financial interest in fighting and this is very important.

[Najm] During the battles that raged in Afghanistan between the government forces and the Mujahidin, Usamah Bin-Ladin visited Afghanistan several times. During these visits, his participation in the operations with the mujahidin developed from one level to the next.

[Bin-Ladin] This military camp was called the al-Ansar Lions' Den, or the Arab camp. In 1987, it was exposed to land and air attacks from the Soviet and Afghan communist government forces against the Arab camps at the time. The Afghan fighters who were there withdrew when the battles, the air attacks, and the landing of paratroopers began. The Arab fighters, led by Shaykh 'Abdallah 'Azzam and Usamah Bin-Muhammad Bin-Ladin and a group that, as far as we knew, did not exceed 35 persons, held their ground for two weeks of fierce fighting. Then the so-called legend of Bin-Ladin or the Arab fighters in Afghanistan was born and began to develop gradually, especially ... [sentence incomplete; voice fades out]

[Najm] This was Usamah Bin-Ladin's experience that was accumulated in years of fighting. An experience of which he is proud because he believes it ended with a victory over the Soviets, an experience he used to establish a training camp which was attacked by the United States with missiles. The United States called this camp the "base camp."

[Najm] Two main characters were the driving force behind receiving and organizing Arab fighters and then sending them to the battlefield. They were Shaykh 'Abdallah 'Azzam, a Palestinian shaykh who decided to undertake jihad, and Usamah Bin-Ladin.

[Begin recording of Shaykh 'Azzam's voice over video clip of tanks firing, battle scenes, piles of ammunition, scenes of destruction, and the 1996 house and camp of Bin-Ladin]

To the widowed mothers, orphaned children, our righteous martyrs, makers of glory, and leaders of conquests, we present this tape entitled: The buzzing of bullets. [Bin-Ladin] Shaykh 'Abdallah 'Azzam, may God have mercy on his soul, is a man worth a nation. After his assassination, Muslim women proved to be unable to give birth to a man like him. The people of jihad who lived that epoch know that Islamic Jihad in Afghanistan has not benefited from anyone as it has from Shaykh 'Abdallah 'Azzam. He instigated the nation from the farthest east to the farthest west. During that blessed jihad, the activities of Shaykh 'Abdallah 'Azzam, may god bless his soul, as well as the activities of our brother mujahidin in Palestine, particularly Hamas, increased. His books, particularly his book The Verses of the Merciful, began to enter Palestine and instigate the nation for jihad against the Jews. The shaykh proceeded from the narrow, regional, and often city atmosphere that was familiar to Islamists and shaykhs, to the larger Islamic world and began to instigate this Islamic world. We and the shaykh were in one boat, as is known to you, together with our brother Wa'il Jalidan.

A plot was concocted to assassinate all. We were very careful not to be together all the time. I often asked the shaykh, may God have mercy on his soul, to stay away from Peshawar in (Sada) due to the increasing plots, especially since one or two weeks earlier a bomb was discovered in the mosque where the shaykh lived in Sab' al-Layl. The Jews were mostly harmed by Shaykh 'Abdallah 'Azzam's movement. It is believed that Israel, together with some of its Arab agents, were the ones who assassinated the shaykh. As for this accusation, I think that it is being promoted today by the Jews, Americans, and some of their agents. However, this is not worth a response. It is illogical for a person to chop off his head and the one who was in the field knows the extent of the strong relationship between me and Shaykh 'Abdallah 'Azzam. This accusation is silly and baseless. There was no competition [between me and him]. Shaykh 'Abdallah's field was that of call [da'wah] and instigation, while we were on the (Baktia) mountains in the interior. He sent us young people as well as directives. We did what he ordered us. We pray that God will accept him and his two sons, Muhammad and Ibrahim, as martyrs, and to compensate the nation by giving it one who can carry out the duty he used to perform.

[Ibrahim] This was a phenomenon that was considered healthy by all those opposing occupation and colonialism, even if this colonialism was by a friendly state like the Soviet Union at that time. When the Soviet occupation of Afghanistan came to an end, a large number of the volunteers maintained fighting as part of their lifestyle. They diverted their attention from fighting a non-Muslim foreign occupier to an attempt to topple regimes in Arab and Islamic states, which they did not consider sufficiently Islamic. Those Arab nationals were called the Afghan Arabs or Arab Afghans. Some of them returned to Algeria, Egypt, Yemen, and other states and tried to do so. They originally came from middle-class society and had some degree of knowledge and education. They had an ambition to be something in this life through public service, educational excellence, or vocational prominence. When they faced obstacles to the attainment of their ambition, which I think was legitimate, they either left their country in search of other opportunities abroad, or began to question the legitimacy of the regime, which does not allow them to fulfill this legitimate ambition.

[Valyenkov, commander of Russian ground troops in Afghanistan during the Russian invasion of the country] We evacuated Afghanistan in circumstances that I vividly remember, because I was there. There were lots of flowers. Similarly, the people were tearful. Of course, this was not the sentiment of all Afghans. For those who were hurt by the war or suffered a setback as a result of it had completely different sentiments. Nonetheless, most Afghans had fears about the repercussions of our withdrawal from the country. They even tried to obstruct this withdrawal. If we are to talk about Afghan leaders, they did not want this at all. I am talking about Najibullah and others. [video footage from archives shows hostilities in the Afghan war]

[Najm] The Soviets left. They withdrew after it had become clear that Afghanistan was a quagmire that drowned the Soviet Union in stagnant political and military waters. The entire Soviet empire was about to collapse. The mujahidin felt victorious and proud, because they felt that they brought the greatest military power on earth to its knees. They waged the war and won it. An enemy was vanquished while another is still to be overcome.

[Bin-Ladin] Nowadays, jihad needs to be waged by the nation. The obligation to engage in jihad may be dropped if people suffer from disability. But, we believe that those who participated in the jihad in Afghanistan bear the greatest responsibility in this regard, because they realized that with insignificant capabilities, with a small number of RPG's, with a small number of antitank mines, with a small number of Kalashnikov rifles, they managed to crush the greatest empire known to mankind. They crushed the greatest military machine. The so-called superpowers vanished into thin air. We think that the United States is very much weaker than Russia. Based on the reports we received from our brothers who participated in jihad in Somalia, we learned that they saw the weakness, frailty, and cowardice of US troops. Only 80 US troops were killed. Nonetheless, they fled in the heart of darkness, frustrated, after they had caused great commotion about the new world order.

[Jamal Isma'il, al-Jazirah correspondent who conducted an interview with Bin-Ladin] Until the year 1989, he [Bin-Ladin] was in Peshawar or in Afghanistan in general. He used to frequent Peshawar. Afterwards, he left for the Kingdom of Saudi Arabia on a visit. He was denied travel for domestic reasons. However, the former Pakistani government said that this had something to do with the Pakistani Government, which asked that he be deported from Pakistani territory.

[Najm] A short while after his return to Saudi Arabia, the region was boiling with change. The following year, the earthquake occurred. [video shows footage from the archives of the Iraqi-Kuwaiti crisis]

[Former US President George Bush] We're here to protect freedom, we're here to protect our future, and we're here to protect innocent lives. But we won't pull punches, we are not here on some exercise. This is a real world situation. And we are not walking away until our mission is done, until the invader is out of Kuwait. And that may well be where you come in. [Gulf War footage from archives]

[Najm] Arab Afghans began to return to their home countries at almost the same time. Since that date, their presence was felt in several Arab capitals which pointed a finger of accusation at them regarding many operations which extremist Islamic groups were accused of. In Algeria, in Egypt, in Saudi Arabia, and many of them appeared in the United Kingdom.

[Isma'il] After the second Gulf war, the war of Kuwait, Usamah Bin-Ladin was given a passport by the Saudi Government -- and at the time he was not permitted to have a passport -- with an exit-only visa. The following day, he left for the Pakistani city of Peshawar. At the time, his movement and activity was engulfed with some secrecy in fear of being exposed to assassination, especially since Shaykh 'Abdallah 'Azzam was assassinated in Peshawar with his two sons Muhammad and Ibrahim two years earlier.

[Bin-Ladin] We were in deep grief during the dispute between these factions and the parties of the Mujahidin. But God Almighty was gracious to the Arab nations by giving it the Taleban Movement, which came to rescue this Jihad from the US scheme which supported Najib

110

[Najibullah] and was pressuring the Mujahidin, through Pakistan, to form a secular government. Fifty percent of its members would be former communists and some of those who had studied in the west, and the rest would be from the seven Afghan parties.

Praise be to God, we were blessed with the coming of this movement. It came at a time when things came to a head and people got sick and tired of bandits of which there were becoming more and more, unfortunately. The Americans and their allies managed to divide Afghanistan to five small states. You, in Pakistan, no doubt are watching this. There was a state in the east, which is called (Hawzat Sharq), Jalalabad. They are (Ningirhar) (Lughman) and (Kunar). There was a state and a president of a state. Their leader was Haji Qadir. In the west there was another state, there was a state and a president of a state led by Haji Qadir. In the West there was another state, (Hawzat Gharb). Muhammad Isma'il Khan and he ruled over three to four provinces between (Hirat), (Farah), and Numrouz) and that too was a virtually independent government from Afghanistan. In the north there was the state that was supported by the communists in the past and it was led by Dostum. He had provinces there. In the north and the center there was a government ruled by Ahmad Shah Mas'ud and Najib and Sayyaf.

What is shocking is that every time Muslims are deceived. How can we believe that a government can be established in Kabul and in one neighborhood we have, Najib the communist who killed more than 70,000 Muslims, and right next to him there is Ahmad Shah Mas'ud? How can we believe that they had a joint government in the full sense of the word and that the former communist president Najib signs the state budget? Then we are told: We are not Communists and we do not support the communists. In reality, it was a joint government being supported by foreign parties and Najib was part of it.

The southern part was a state for the Taleban. It consists of the provinces of Qandahar, Zabol, and (Hilmend). So there were five governments in this small state, not to mention the bandits who were considered small states with the states.

God blessed the Muslims with the coming of the Taleban rule. It was not a force being pushed in from abroad, as the Crusaders in the western media try to depict them; but it was rather a pulling force from the inside. People had become sick and tired of road bandits and from paying taxes and protection money. So any tribe that had students of religion who had connections with the Taleban they [the Taleban] would ask the students to come to this or that province. This is why we see that engineer Hekmatyar was on the borders of Kabul for four years. He had the public support of Pakistan and was trying to move forward a few meters to seize Kabul, but he could not. It is known that the Islamic party led by Hekmatyar is the best Afghan party in terms of power, organization, and deployment in Afghanistan. He could not move forward. On the other hand, it is also known, these students of religion are generally young and many of them had not participated in fighting. But because of the popular support after the people had reached a state of despair from previous events, they were successful.

[Hekmatyar] I honestly think that this war was forced on us just like these wars were imposed on all the Muslims in the world. I ask you: Why are all the wars taking place in the Muslim world? Why are Muslims being killed and their houses destroyed? Why are the problems in Europe and the United States easily solved, while simple issues in the Muslim world ignite vicious wars? Why the problems in Algeria, Palestine, and Kashmir? I think that the Hizb-e Islami is the underdog. Unfortunately, the Muslim world does not know how this war was imposed, starting with the war that the coalition government in Kabul declared against the Hizb-e Islami and later the Taleban Movement.

Why does the US State Department say: We are the ones who did not permit Hekmatyar to enter Kabul? The US defense minister said: We cannot allow the Hizb-e Islami to rule Kabul; while a CIA official tells CNN: We have decided to destroy the Hizb-e Islami. This is what they say, but there are people who do not know how the war started, who is funding it, and why it is being launched against the Hizb-e Islami, or why the coalition government and later the Taleban movement are waging a war against the party. The United States was behind this war just to prove to everyone that Jihad is a failure. If an Islamic government was formed by the mujahidin after the collapse of the Soviet Union, the United States believed that this type of government will spread to the rest of the rest of the region. They thought to themselves: We must strike at this movement and not allow the mujahidin to form an Islamic government. They consequently imposed this war on us.

[Isma'il] In 1991 and 1992, I interviewed him [Bin-Ladin] more than once to find out some details. At that time I was a correspondent for [London-based] Al-Hayah newspaper and he was the head of a reconciliation committee between the Afghan factions that were at war in some states. He was chosen by these factions as a neutral party that is supportive of Afghan jihad in general. After 1992, when the mujahidin parties entered the Afghan capital, Kabul, and were at war with each other, which stunned all observers, especially the Muslims, Usamah Bin-Ladin -- along with a number of Arab Islamic activists who were in Peshawar and other Arab countries -- exerted intensive mediation efforts between Hekmatyar, Masud, and Rabbani, but all these efforts failed, so he moved to Sudan in mid-1992 and stayed there until May 1996, when the Sudanese Government was forced to ask him to leave.

According to the Afghan information minister in the Taleban Government, a deal was made between the United States and Sudan to drive Usamah Bin-Ladin out to Afghanistan because Afghanistan has no means of communication. In return for this, the sanctions and economic and political pressure on Sudan was to be eased off.

['Atwan] He [Bin-Ladin] told me about attempts to tempt him to stop his jihad and the money he was offered. He said -- and he was telling the truth -- that he was offered hundreds of millions of dollars and he refused them. He named the mediators who visited him, whether in Sudan or even in Afghanistan, to talk him into going back, and he refused. He used to affirm that he will stick with this approach until the end and that he has dedicated his life to the cause of God and Islam. He was saying this without hesitation.

He told me about his days in Sudan and the challenge he faced when Arab aid to Sudan stopped and how he was able to survive with limited local resources. He told me about the agricultural projects he carried out in the al-Jazirah area in Sudan. He told me that this country can feed the whole world if it were allowed to be properly invested. He told me about how he was able to produce a record number of sunflowers. His agricultural projects were many and included cotton farms. He wished he could have stayed in Sudan and continued his projects, but he was forced to flee back to Afghanistan.

[Najm] In 1994, we saw the first attack against US targets in the Middle East begin. The target was Riyadh, the headquarters of the US mission which was training the Saudi National Guard. In 1996, an attack was carried out in al-Khubar, the headquarters of the US Marine force. Some reports linked both with Usamah Bin-Ladin, who made every effort to praise the men who carried out the attacks.

[Bin-Ladin] These were popular reactions by young men who willingly offered their lives, seeking the satisfaction of Almighty God. I hold in great esteem and respect these great men because they removed the brand of shame from the forehead of our [Islamic] nation, whether those who carried out attacks in Riyadh or those who carried out bombing attacks in al-Khubar and East Africa and other places. I also view with great esteem our brother cubs in Palestine who are teaching the Jews lessons in faith and the pride of the faithful. Regrettably, after these daring operations in Palestine, the world's infidelity was gathered. It is a cause of sadness that they gathered on the soil of Egypt. They gathered their agents from the rulers of the region, the Arab rulers, who had been deceiving the Islamic nation for more than half a century. Whenever a president and a king met they used to say that they discussed the Palestinian cause. Fifty years later, the clear picture emerged; namely, they met not only to betray the mujahidin in Palestine but to denounce these cubs whose fathers and brothers were killed, imprisoned, and tortured in defense of their religion and for endeavoring to evacuate the infidels from their land. The proverb says: Clear things are impossible to explain.

['Abd-al-Bari 'Atwan, chief editor of the London-based Arabic daily Al-Quds al-'Arabi] Following the attacks on the US forces in al-Khubar and in Riyadh, he [Bin-Ladin] expressed unusual sympathy with those who carried out the attacks. He was very close to saying that they were from among his supporters. He was close but he did not say this. You sense pride in his eyes, that these real men, as he told me, were capable of implementing these two successful operations.

[Najm] However, the real turning point which drew the attention of the United States was the issuance of a fatwa [religious edict].

[Bin-Ladin] The previous fatwa says that in our religion, we have divisions that are different from what they claim, even if they claim something and act in the opposite way. We differentiate between the man, the woman, the child, and the old people. The man is a fighter, whether he carries arms or helps kill us by paying taxes and by gathering information. He is a fighter. With regards to reports among Muslims that 'Usamah is threatening to kill civilians, then, what are they killing

115

in Palestine? They are killing children, not only civilians, but children as well. The United States has an advantage media-wise and has great media power that varies its standards according to its needs. Our enemy, the target -- if God gives Muslims the opportunity to do so -- is every American male, whether he is directly fighting us or paying taxes.

You may have heard these days that almost three quarters of the US people support Clifton's strikes on Iraq. They are a people whose president becomes more popular when he kills innocent people. They are a people who increase their support for their president when he commits some of the seven cardinal sins. They are a lowly people who do not understand the meaning of principles.

As I said, we are pursuing our rights to have them [the Americans] evicted from the Muslim world countries and to prevent them from dominating us. We believe that the right to self-defense is to be enjoyed by all people. Israel is stockpiling hundreds of nuclear warheads and bombs. The Christian West is largely in possession of such weapons. Hence, we do not regard this as a charge, but rather as a right. We do not accept to see anybody level charges against us in this regard. It is as if you were accusing a man of being a courageous knight and fighter. It is as if you were denying him this. Only a man who is not in his right mind would level such accusations. This is a right. We supported the Pakistani people and congratulated them when God was gracious enough to enable them to acquire the nuclear weapon. We regard this as one of our rights, of Muslim rights. We disregard such worn-out US charges.

Let us say that there are two parties to the conflict: The first party is world Christianity, which is allied with Zionist Jewry and led by the United States, Britain, and Israel; while the second party is the Muslim world. In such a conflict, it is unacceptable to see the first party mount attacks, desecrate my lands and holy shrines, and plunder the Muslims' oil. When it is met by any resistance on the part of the Muslims, this party brands the Muslims as terrorists. This is stupidity. People's intelligence is being belittled. We believe that it is our religious duty to resist this occupation with all the power that we have and to punish it using the same means it is pursuing against us.

The US claims are numerous. If we presume that they are true, we are not concerned by them. These people are resisting the forces of world infidelity that occupied their lands. Why should the United States get angry when the people resist its aggressions? Its claims are baseless. However, if it means that I have something to do with instigating them, I would like to say that this is obvious. I have frequently admitted to having done so. I admitted that I was one of those who cosigned the fatwa [religious edict] that urged the nation to engage in jihad. We did so a few years ago. Thanks be to God, many people responded favorably to our fatwa. Of these people were the brothers whom we regard as martyrs. They were brother 'Abd-al-'Aziz al-Mi'thim, who was killed in Riyadh, brother Muslih al-Shamrani, brother Riyad al-Hajiri, and brother Khalid al-Sa'id. The only strength is that bestowed by God. We beseech Almighty God to accept them all. During interrogation, they admitted to coming under the influence of some of the statements and circulars we issued to people. In these statements and circulars, we communicated the *Fatwas* issued by clergymen regarding the need to engage in jihad against these US occupiers.

['Atwan] I felt that the man had his own vision and special strategy. This strategy is based on his concept of the region. The first point in this strategy is that the US Administration or the US forces, which he considers occupation forces in the Gulf and Arabian Peninsula, are a prelude to a comprehensive Israeli-Jewish hegemony over the region with the aim of looting its wealth and humiliating its Muslim people. One senses this as the essence of his creed and strategy. Therefore, he believes that expelling these US forces from the Arab world is a top priority. He believes that the regimes should be reformed or, more correctly, changed. The regimes immune to reform should be changed, the shari'ah should be applied properly, and a just Islamic system should be set up in the Islamic and Arab states, particularly the Gulf States. This is a summary of his strategy. Currently, he does not want to fight the regimes. That is what he told me. He wants to fight the Americans, who are protecting these regimes.

[Najm] Although Usamah Bin-Ladin insists in all his statements that his role is confined to the issuance of *Fatwas* and instigation, he almost stated in the interview conducted with him by our correspondent Jamal Isma'il that he was aware of all aspects of the US Embassy explosion in Nairobi.

[Bin-Ladin] It was a painful blow. They [the Americans] had not sustained such a blow since the blowing up of the Marines in Lebanon. The Nairobi [US] Embassy was actually six embassies combined in one. The brutal US invasion of Somalia kicked off from there. Some 13,000 from among our brothers, women, and sons in Somalia were killed under the banner of the United Nations. Reports, corroborated by photographs, said that our Somali brothers were grilled as if they were sheep. It is only God who bestows strength. They did not speak about the scope of brutality or aggression and so forth and so on. Muslims are always reproached when they defend themselves. For the past few decades, plots have been hatched to partition Sudan from there. These plots are hatched in Nairobi. As is widely known, the US Embassy in Nairobi is the agency that is doing this. The greatest CIA center in eastern Africa is located at this embassy. Thanks to God's grace to Muslims, the blow was successful and great. They deserved it. It made them taste what we tasted during the massacres committed in Sabra, Shatila, Dayr Yasin, Qana, Hebron, and elsewhere.

[Najm] The United States did not make do with the bombardment. It issued an arrest warrant against Usamah Bin-Ladin and promised a $5 million prize to whoever provides information leading to his arrest. It tried to freeze his financial assets. Usamah Bin-Ladin began his odyssey in Afghanistan when he was 22 years old. Now, he is 42 years old. He was the paramount Arab Afghan. The number of Arab Afghans in Afghanistan is diminishing. Those who met him said that he is no longer the same man.

['Atwan] I believe that the Nairobi and Dar es Salam bombings changed Bin-Ladin. He was aware that the Americans were targeting him, but not with this intensity. There was not a single piece of evidence that he was behind the al-Khubar and Riyadh bombings. He may have been wanted by the Americans. But, there was no powerful evidence incriminating him. I think that the situation now is different. Nonetheless, even prior to these two incidents, the man took all the necessary security precautions. For example, I know that he built a camp in the open air to give the impression that it was his base when he was interviewed by CNN. It was not a base. I am aware of this. He did not allow the CNN team to bring its own camera. The team left for the camp and found the camera waiting for it. It was Bin-Ladin's camera. He asked the team members not to bring anything with them. The CNN team members were inspected, pursued, and monitored indirectly to make sure that they were neither followed nor monitored by the US intelligence service. The man knows how to take care of his security concerns. I hope that he will be successful in his efforts in this regard. He is taking his own precautions. I know that he is now in a secure place, that his moves are banned, not because Taleban wants to restrain his moves, but because it wants to protect him. Taleban officials have strong convictions that the press and press men are the trap that could track his whereabouts and bring about his liquidation.

[Isma'il] It goes without saying that he feels that is under siege. He as well as the Afghan Taleban-led government admitted that his moves in Afghanistan are not restrained. Nonetheless, he is banned from engaging in any action originating in Afghan territory against any country whatsoever regardless of whether or not it has recognized the Taleban-led government. All that he is currently doing on Afghan territory is confined to addressing appeals, engaging in media-related activities, and issuing *Fatwas*, along with a group of Afghan or other clergymen, promoting fighting, which Taleban cannot ban or restrain, because this is enshrined in Koranic verses and traditions of the prophet.

[Najm] The base was destroyed, but Bin-Ladin survived. He is trying to mobilize more supporters even though he has fears that their number may shrink in the future.

[Bin-Ladin] When jihad was obscured for a long time, we saw the emergence of a generation of students who did not experience the heat of jihad. They were affected by the US media that invaded Islamic countries. Without even engaging in combat, they suffered a psychological defeat. They acknowledge the necessity for jihad. Nonetheless, they say that they cannot fulfill such an obligation. The people who had the honor of engaging in jihad in Afghanistan, Bosnia-Herzevogina, or Chechnya-- we had such an honor--are certain that the nation nowadays can, God willing, engage in jihad against the enemies of Islam, particularly, the external archenemy, the Crusader-Jewish alliance.

[Najm] All this brings us back to the Arabian Gulf, which some call the Persian Gulf. Shiites are living on one of its coasts, while the other coast is inhabited by a combination of Sunnites and Shiites. Holy shrines are located to the west of the gulf: In Mecca, Medina, and Jerusalem. Similarly, holy shrines are located to the north: In al-Najaf and Karbala'. There are also holy shrines in the east: In Qom and Mashhad. Afghanistan is a stone's throw away. Iraq is under siege.

Weapons are deployed at sea, on land, and in the air. An oil artery is running through its waters. It is the embodiment of wealth and conflict. What we forget in the midst of routine details is the cumulative effect of things. When somebody drops a stone in a river, this may cause the river course to change once and for all. Washington and Usamah Bin-Ladin are part of this mosaic. To them, the targets have been delineated and the pursuit has begun."

September 28, 2001. Interview published in *Ummat* Karachi newspaper.[72]

UMMAT: You have been accused of involvement in the attacks in New York and Washington. What do you want to say about this? If you are not involved, who might be?

USAMA BIN LADEN: In the name of Allah (God), the most beneficent, the most merciful. Praise be to Allah, Who is the creator of the whole universe and Who made the Earth as an abode for peace, for the whole humankind. Allah is the Sustainer, who sent Prophet Muhammad (peace be upon him) for our guidance. I am thankful to the Ummat Group of Publications, which gave me the opportunity to convey my viewpoint to the people, particularly the valiant and momin (true Muslim) people of Pakistan who refused to believe the lies of the demon (Pakistani military dictator General Pervez Musharraf).

I have already said that I am not involved in the 11 September attacks in the United States. As a Muslim, I try my best to avoid telling a lie. I had no knowledge of these attacks, nor do I consider the killing of innocent women, children and other humans as an appreciable act. Islam strictly forbids causing harm to innocent women, children and other people. Such a practice is forbidden even in the course of a battle. It is the United States, which is perpetrating every maltreatment on women, children and common people of other faiths, particularly the followers of Islam. All that is going on in Palestine for the last 11 months is sufficient to call the wrath of God upon the United States and Israel. There is also a warning for those Muslim countries, which witnessed all these as a silent spectator. What had earlier been done to the innocent people of Iraq, Chechnya and Bosnia? Only one conclusion could be derived from the indifference of the United States and the West to these acts of terror and the patronage of the tyrants by these powers that America is an anti-Islamic power and it is patronizing the anti-Islamic forces. Its friendship with the Muslim countries is just a show, rather deceit. By enticing or intimidating these countries, the United States is forcing them to play a role of its choice. Put a glance all around and you will see that the slaves of the United States are either rulers or enemies of Muslims.

The U.S. has no friends, nor does it want to keep any because the prerequisite of friendship is to come to the level of the friend or consider him at par with you. America does not want to see anyone equal to it. It expects slavery from others. Therefore, other countries are either its slaves or subordinates. However, our case is different. We have pledged slavery to God Almighty alone and after this pledge there is no possibility to become the slave of someone else. If we do that it will be disregardful to both our Sustainer and his fellow beings. Most of the world nations upholding their freedom are the religious ones, which are the enemies of the United States, or the U.S. itself considers them as its enemies.

The countries which do not agree to become the U.S. slaves are China, Iran, Libya, Cuba, Syria [Afghanistan, Pakistan, Bangladesh, Iraq, Sudan, Indonesia, Malaysia] and Russia. Whoever committed the act of 11 September are not the friends of the American people. I have already said that we are against the American system, not against its people, whereas in these attacks, the common American people have been killed. According to my information, the death toll is much higher than what the U.S. Government has stated. But the Bush Administration does not want the panic to spread. The United States should try to trace the perpetrators of these attacks within itself; the people who are a part of the U.S. system, but are dissenting against it. Or those who are working for some other system; persons who want to make the present century as a century of conflict between Islam and Christianity so that their own civilization, nation, country, or ideology could survive. They can be anyone, from Russia to Israel and from India to Serbia. In the U.S. itself, there are dozens of well-organized and well-equipped groups, which are capable of causing a large-scale destruction. Then you cannot forget the American-Jews, who are annoyed with President Bush ever since the elections in Florida and want to avenge him.

Then there are intelligence agencies in the U.S., which require billions of dollars worth of funds from the Congress and the government every year. This [funding issue] was not a big problem till the existence of the former Soviet Union but after that the budget of these agencies has been in danger. They needed an enemy. So, they first started propaganda against Usama and Taleban and then this incident happened. You see, the Bush Administration approved a budget of 40 billion dollars. Where will this huge amount go? It will be provided to the same agencies, which need huge funds and want to exert their importance. Now they will spend the money for their expansion and for increasing their importance. I will give you an example. Drug smugglers from all over the world are in contact with the U.S. secret agencies. These agencies do not want to eradicate narcotics cultivation and trafficking because their importance will be diminished. The people in the U.S. Drug Enforcement Department are encouraging drug trade so that they could show performance and get millions of dollars worth of budget. General Noriega was made a drug baron by the CIA and, in need, he was made a scapegoat. In the same way, whether it is President Bush or any other U.S. President, they cannot bring Israel to justice for its human rights abuses or to hold it accountable for such crimes. What is this? Is it not that there exists a government within the government in the United Sates? That secret government must be asked as to who carried out the attacks.

UMMAT: A number of world countries have joined the call of the United States for launching attacks on Afghanistan. These also include a number of Muslim countries. Will Al-Qa'idah declare a jihad against these Islamic countries as well?

USAMA BIN LADEN: I must say that my duty is just to awaken the Muslims; to tell them as to what is good for them and what is not. What does Islam say and what do the enemies of Islam want. Al-Qa'idah was set up to wage a jihad against infidelity, particularly to counter the onslaught of the infidel countries against the Islamic states. Jihad is the sixth undeclared pillar of Islam. [The first five being the basic holy words of Islam ("There is no god but God and Muhammad is the messenger of God"), prayers, fasting (in Ramadan), pilgrimage to Mecca and giving alms (zakat).] Every anti-Islamic person is afraid of jihad. Al-Qa'idah wants to keep jihad alive and active and make it a part of the daily life of the Muslims. It wants to give it the status of worship. We are not against any Islamic country. We do not consider a war against an Islamic country as jihad. We are in favour of armed jihad only against those infidel governments, which are killing innocent Muslim men, women and children just because they are Muslims. Supporting the U.S. act is the need of some Muslim countries and the compulsion of others. However, they should think as to what will remain of their religious and moral position if they support the attack of the Christians and the Jews on a Muslim country like Afghanistan. The orders of Islamic Shariah [jurisprudence] for such individuals, organizations and countries are clear and all the scholars of the Muslim brotherhood are unanimous on them. We will do the same, which is being ordered by the Ameer-ul-Momeneen [the commander of the faithful] Muhammad Omar [leader of the Taleban] and the Islamic scholars. The hearts of the people of Muslim countries are beating with the call of jihad. We are grateful to them.

UMMAT: The losses caused in the attacks in New York and Washington have proved that giving an economic blow to the U.S. is not too difficult. U.S. experts admit that a few more such attacks can bring down the American economy. Why is Al-Qa'idah not targeting their economic pillars?

USAMA BIN LADEN: I have already said that we are not hostile to the United States. We are against the [U.S. Government] system, which makes other nations slaves of the United States, or forces them to mortgage their political and economic freedom. This system is totally in the control of the American Jews, whose first priority is Israel, not the United States. It is clear that the American people are themselves the slaves of the Jews and are forced to live according to the principles and laws laid down by them. So the punishment should reach Israel. In fact, it is Israel, which is giving a blood bath to innocent Muslims and the U.S. is not uttering a single word.

UMMAT: Why is harm not caused to the enemies of Islam through other means, apart from the armed struggle? For instance, urging the Muslims to boycott Western products, banks, shipping lines and TV channels.

USAMA BIN LADEN: The first thing is that Western products could only be boycotted when the Muslim fraternity is fully awakened and organized. Secondly, the Muslim companies should become self-sufficient in producing goods equal to the products of Western companies. Economic boycott of the West is not possible unless economic self-sufficiency is attained and substitute products are brought out. You see that wealth is scattered all across the Muslim World but not a single TV channel has been acquired which can preach Islamic injunctions according to modern requirements and attain an international influence. Muslim traders and philanthropists should make it a point that if the weapon of public opinion is to be used, it is to be kept in the hand. Today's world is of public opinion and the fates of nations are determined through its pressure. Once the tools for building public opinion are obtained, everything that you asked for can be done.

UMMAT: The entire propaganda about your struggle has so far been made by the Western media. But no information is being received from your sources about the network of Al-Qa'idah and its jihadi successes. Would you comment?

USAMA BIN LADEN: In fact, the Western media is left with nothing else. It has no other theme to survive for a long time. Then we have many other things to do. The struggle for jihad and the successes are for the sake of Allah and not to annoy His bondsmen. Our silence is our real propaganda. Rejections, explanations, or corrigendum only waste your time and through them, the enemy wants you to engage in things which are not of use to you. These things are pulling you away from your cause. The Western media is unleashing such a baseless propaganda, which makes us surprise but it reflects on what is in their hearts and gradually they themselves become captive of this propaganda. They become afraid of it and begin to cause harm to themselves. Terror is the most dreaded weapon in modern age and the Western media is mercilessly using it against its own people. It can add fear and helplessness in the psyche of the people of Europe and the United States. It means that what the enemies of the United States cannot do, its media is doing that. You can understand as to what will be the performance of the nation in a war, which suffers from fear and helplessness.

UMMAT: What will be the impact of the freeze of Al-Qa'idah accounts by the U.S.?

USAMA BIN LADEN: God opens up ways for those who work for Him. Freezing of accounts will not make any difference for Al-Qa'idah or other jihad groups. With the grace of Allah, Al-Qa'idah has more than three alternative financial systems, which are all separate and totally independent from each other. This system is operating under the patronage of those who love jihad. What to say of the United States, even the combined world cannot budge these people from their path. These people are not in hundreds but in thousands and millions. Al-Qa'idah comprises of such modern educated youths who are aware of the cracks inside the Western financial system as they are aware of the lines in their hands. These are the very flaws of the Western fiscal system, which are becoming a noose for it and this system could not recuperate in spite of the passage of so many days.

UMMAT: Are there other safe areas other than Afghanistan, where you can continue jihad?

USAMA BIN LADEN: There are areas in all parts of the world where strong jihadi forces are present, from Indonesia to Algeria, from Kabul to Chechnya, from Bosnia to Sudan, and from Burma to Kashmir. Then it is not the problem of my person. I am a helpless fellowman of God, constantly in the fear of my accountability before God. It is not the question of Usama but of Islam and, in Islam too, of jihad. Thanks to God, those waging a jihad can walk today with their heads raised. Jihad was still present when there was no Usama and it will remain as such even when Usama is no longer there. Allah opens up ways and creates loves in the hearts of people for those who walk on the path of Allah with their lives, property and children. Believe it, through jihad, a man gets everything he desires. And the biggest desire of a Muslim is the life after death. Martyrdom is the shortest way of attaining an eternal life.

UMMAT: What do you say about the Pakistan Government policy on Afghanistan attack?

USAMA BIN LADEN: We are thankful to the Momin and valiant people of Pakistan who erected a blockade in front of the evil forces and stood in the first file of battle. Pakistan is a great hope for the Islamic brotherhood. Its people are awakened, organized and rich in the spirit of faith. They backed Afghanistan in its war against the Soviet Union and extended every help to the mojahedeen (freedom fighters) and the Afghan people. Then these are very Pakistanis who are standing shoulder by shoulder with the Taleban. If such people emerge in just two countries, the domination of the West will diminish in a matter of days. Our hearts beat with Pakistan and, God forbid, if a difficult time comes we will protect it with our blood. Pakistan is sacred for us like a place of worship. We are the people of jihad and fighting for the defense of Pakistan is the best of all jihads to us. It does not matter for us as to who reforms Pakistan. The important thing is that the spirit of jihad is alive and stronger in the hearts of the Pakistani people.

End of Interview"

October, 2001. Tayseer Alouni, Al-Jazeera television correspondent, interview with Osama Bin Laden. Translated by CNN. [73]

"TAYSEER ALOUNI: Dear viewers, welcome to this much-anticipated interview with the leader of the al Qaeda organization, Sheikh Osama Bin Laden.

Sheikh, the question that's on the mind of many people around the world: America claims that it has convincing evidence of your collusion in the events in New York and Washington. What's your answer?

OSAMA BIN LADEN: America has made many accusations against us and many other Muslims around the world. Its charge that we are carrying out acts of terrorism is an unwarranted description.

We never heard in our lives a court decision to convict someone based on a "secret" proof it has. The logical thing to do is to present a proof to a court of law. What many leaders have said so far is that America has an indication only, and not a tangible proof. They describe those brave guys who took the battle to the heart of America and destroyed its most famous economic and military landmarks.

They did this, as we understand it, and this is something we have agitated for before, as a matter of self-defense, in defense of our brothers and sons in Palestine, and to liberate our sacred religious sites/things. If inciting people to do that is terrorism, and if killing those who kill our sons is terrorism, then let history be witness that we are terrorists.

Q: Sheikh, those who follow your statements and speeches may link your threats to what happened in America. To quote one of your latest statements: "I swear that America won't enjoy security before we live it for real in Palestine." It is easy for anyone following developments to link the acts to your threats.

BIN LADEN: It is easy to link them.

We have agitated for this for years and we have issued statements and *Fatwas* to that effect. This appeared in the investigations into the four young men who destroyed the American center in Ulayya in Riyadh, as disclosed and published by the Saudi government. The [Saudis] reported that they were influenced by some of the *Fatwas* and statements that we issued. Also, apart from that, incitement continues in many meetings and has been published in the media. If they mean, or if you mean, that there is a link as a result of our incitement, then it is true. We incite because incitement is our [unintelligible] today. God assigned incitement to the best of all mankind, Mohammed, who said, "Fight for the sake of God. Assign this to no one but yourself, and incite the faithful."

[Bin Laden recites verses from the Quran.]

This is a true response. We have incited battle against Americans and Jews. This is true.

Q: Al Qaeda is facing now a country that leads the world militarily, politically, technologically. Surely, the al Qaeda organization does not have the economic means that the United States has. How can al Qaeda defeat America militarily?

BIN LADEN: This battle is not between al Qaeda and the U.S. This is a battle of Muslims against the global crusaders. In the past when al Qaeda fought with the mujahedeen, we were told, "Wow, can you defeat the Soviet Union?" The Soviet Union scared the whole world then. NATO used to tremble of fear of the Soviet Union. Where is that power now? We barely remember it. It broke down into many small states and Russia remained.

God, who provided us with his support and kept us steadfast until the Soviet Union was defeated, is able to provide us once more with his support to defeat America on the same land and with the same people. We believe that the defeat of America is possible, with the help of God, and is even easier for us, God permitting, than the defeat of the Soviet Union was before.

Q: How can you explain that?

BIN LADEN: We experienced the Americans through our brothers who went into combat against them in Somalia, for example. We found they had no power worthy of mention. There was a huge aura over America -- the United States -- that terrified people even before they entered combat. Our brothers who were here in Afghanistan tested them, and together with some of the mujahedeen in Somalia, God granted them victory. America exited dragging its tails in failure, defeat, and ruin, caring for nothing.

America left faster than anyone expected. It forgot all that tremendous media fanfare about the new world order, that it is the master of that order, and that it does whatever it wants. It forgot all of these propositions, gathered up its army, and withdrew in defeat, thanks be to God. We experienced combat against the Russians for 10 years, from 1979 to 1989, thanks be to God. Then we continued against the communists in Afghanistan. Today, we're at the end of our second week. There is no comparison between the two battles, between this group and that. We pray to God to give us his support and to make America ever more reluctant. God is capable of that.

Q: You said you want to defeat America on this land. Don't you think that the presence of al Qaeda on Afghanistan soil is costing the Afghan people a high price?

BIN LADEN: This is a partial point of view. When we came to Afghanistan to support the mujahedeen in 1979, against the Russians, the Saudi government asked me officially not to enter Afghanistan due to how close my family is to the Saudi leadership. They ordered me to stay in Peshawar, because in the event the Russians arrested me that will be a proof of our support of the mujahedeen against the Soviet Union. At that time, the whole world was scared of the Soviet Union. I didn't obey their order. They thought my entry into Afghanistan was damning to them. I didn't listen to them and I went into Afghanistan for the first time.

We sacrificed a lot in order to keep the Muslim faith alive and save the children. This is a duty for every Muslim, in general, not the Afghans especially. If I run to the rescue of my brothers in Palestine, it doesn't mean it's Osama's duty alone. This is a duty of all Muslims. The jihad is a duty for everyone, not just for the Afghans. The Afghans are suffering, that's true, but this is their Islamic duty. As far as the bombing of Afghanistan, this is not a personal vendetta. America didn't take my money or hurt me in any way. The bombing is a direct effect of our inciting against the Jews and the Americans.

America is against the establishment of any Islamic government. The prophet has said, "They will be target because of their religion." Not because Osama bin Laden is there. When I came here the first time it was because of a desire to revive the Muslim spirit and an attempt at rescuing the children and the powerless. The British attacked Afghanistan before Osama bin Laden was here, Russians came here before me and now the Americans. We pray that god will defeat them just like he did their allies before them. We ask God to give us the power to defeat them as we did others before.

Q: Let's get back to what happened in New York and Washington. What is your assessment of the attacks on America? What's their effect on America and the Muslim world?

BIN LADEN: The events of Tuesday, September the 11th, in New York and Washington are great on all levels. Their repercussions are not over. Although the collapse of the twin towers is huge, but the events that followed, and I'm not just talking about the economic repercussions, those are continuing, the events that followed are dangerous and more enormous than the collapse of the towers.

The values of this Western civilization under the leadership of America have been destroyed. Those awesome symbolic towers that speak of liberty, human rights, and humanity have been destroyed. They have gone up in smoke.

The proof came when the U.S. government pressured the media not to run our statements that are not longer than very few minutes. They felt that the truth started to reach the American people, the truth that we are not terrorists as they understand it but because we are being attacked in Palestine, Iraq, Lebanon, Sudan, Somalia, Kashmir, the Philippines and everywhere else. They understood the truth that this is a reaction from the youth of the Muslim nation against the British government. They forgot all about fair and objective reporting and reporting the other side of the issue. I tell you freedom and human rights in America are doomed. The U.S. government will lead the American people and the West in general will enter an unbearable hell and a choking life because the Western leadership acts under the Zionist lobby's influence for the purpose of serving Israel, which kills our sons unlawfully in order for them to remain in their leadership positions.

Q: What is your assessment of the Arabic reaction and the effects on the Islamic world? Some were joyous. Others said, "We can't accept this. This is terrorism, not Islam."

BIN LADEN: The events proved the extent of terrorism that America exercises in the world. Bush stated that the world has to be divided in two: Bush and his supporters, and any country that doesn't get into the global crusade is with the terrorists. What terrorism is clearer than this? Many governments were forced to support this "new terrorism." They had to go along with this although they knew that we are defending our brothers and defending our sacred values. Many Western and Eastern leaders have said that the true roots of terrorism should be dealt with; they meant the Palestinian cause. Then we have a righteous cause, but they couldn't admit this out loud of fear of America. They say we are terrorists but solve the Palestinian cause. All of a sudden, Bush and Blair declared, "The time has come to establish an independent state for Palestine." Throughout the past years the time hasn't come, until after these attacks, for the establishment of the Palestinian state. They only understand the language of attacks and killings.

Just as they're killing us, we have to kill them so that there will be a balance of terror. This is the first time the balance of terror has been close between the two parties, between Muslims and Americans, in the modern age. American politicians used to do whatever they wanted with us. The victim was forbidden to scream or to moan. [unintelligible]

Clinton has said, "Israel has the right to defend itself," after the massacres of Qana. He didn't even reprimand Israel. When the new President Bush and Colin Powell declared in the first few months of their taking office that they will move the American embassy to Jerusalem. They said Jerusalem will be the eternal capital of Israel. They got a standing ovation in Congress and the Senate. This is the biggest bigotry, and this is tyranny loud and clear.

The battle has moved to inside America. We will work to continue this battle, God permitting, until victory or until we meet God before that occurs.

Q: Sheikh, I see that most of your answers are about Palestine and the Palestinian cause. In the beginning, your focus on killing the unfaithful and the Jews ... and you specified then that the Americans should be sent out of the Arabian Peninsula. Now you're turning your attention to Palestine first and the Arabian Peninsula second. What's your comment?

BIN LADEN: Jihad is a duty to liberate Al-Aqsa, and to help the powerless in Palestine, Iraq and Lebanon and in every Muslim country. There is no doubt that the liberation of the Arabian Peninsula from infidels is a duty as well. But it is not right to say that Osama put the Palestinian issue first. I have given speeches in which I encourage Muslims to boycott America economically. I said Americans take our money and give it to Israel to kill our children in Palestine. I established a front a few years ago named The Islamic Front for Jihad against the Jews and the Crusaders. Sometimes we find the right elements to push for one cause more than the other. Last year's blessed intifada helped us to push more for the Palestinian issue. This push helps the other cause. Attacking America helps the cause of Palestine and vice versa. No conflict between the two; on the contrary, one serves the other.

Q: Sheikh, now let's talk about Christians and Jews. You issued a fatwa for jihad against the Christians and the Jews. As we can see, some other clerics also issued *Fatwas*. There might be some who share your views, and some who oppose them and said this is against the teachings of Islam They ask how can you kill a Jew or a Christian or a Catholic just because of his religion? They say that your statements contradict what Muslim clerics teach.

BIN LADEN: God bless Allah, many *Fatwas* have been declared on these issues, especially in Pakistan. Sami Zai in Pakistan is a very well known authority on this. He has written many times on the subject. So did the famous Abdullah bin Ohkmah Al-Shehebi of Saudi Arabia. I read a book titled "The Truth About The New Crusades." They all wrote about and allowed the fighting of Americans and Israelis in Palestine and allowing their killings and destroying their economies and properties.

Q [interrupting]: How about the killing of innocent civilians?

BIN LADEN: The killing of innocent civilians, as America and some intellectuals claim, is really very strange talk. Who said that our children and civilians are not innocent and that shedding their blood is justified? That it is lesser in degree? When we kill their innocents, the entire world from east to west screams at us, and America rallies its allies, agents, and the sons of its agents. Who said that our blood is not blood, but theirs is? Who made this pronouncement? Who has been getting killed in our countries for decades? More than 1 million children, more than 1 million children died in Iraq and others are still dying. Why do we not hear someone screaming or condemning, or even someone's words of consolation or condolence?

How come millions of Muslims are being killed? Where are the experts, the writers, the scholars and the freedom fighters, where are the ones who have an ounce a faith in them? They react only if we kill American civilians, and every day we are being killed, children are being killed in Palestine. We should review the books. Human nature makes people stand with the powerful without noticing it. When they talk about us, they know we won't respond to them. In the past, an Arab king once killed an ordinary Arab man. The people started wondering how come kings have the right to kill people just like that. Then the victim's brother went and killed the king in revenge. People were disappointed with the young man and asked him, "How could you kill a king for your brother?" The man said, "My brother is my king." We consider all our children in Palestine to be kings.

We kill the kings of the infidels, kings of the crusaders, and civilian infidels in exchange for those of our children they kill. This is permissible in law and intellectually.

Q: So what you are saying is that this is a type of reciprocal treatment. They kill our innocents, so we kill their innocents.

BIN LADEN: So we kill their innocents, and I say it is permissible in law and intellectually, because those who spoke on this matter spoke from a juridical perspective.

Q: What is their position?

BIN LADEN: That it is not permissible. They spoke of evidence that the Messenger of God forbade the killing of women and children. This is true.

[Break in tape.]

Q: This is exactly what I'm asking about.

BIN LADEN: However, this prohibition of the killing of children and innocents is not absolute. It is not absolute. There are other texts that restrict it.

I agree that the Prophet Mohammed forbade the killing of babies and women. That is true, but this is not absolute. There is a saying, "If the infidels killed women and children on purpose, we shouldn't shy way from treating them in the same way to stop them from doing it again." The men that God helped [attack, on September 11] did not intend to kill babies; they intended to destroy the strongest military power in the world, to attack the Pentagon that houses more than 64,000 employees, a military center that houses the strength and the military intelligence.

Q: How about the twin towers?

BIN LADEN: The towers are an economic power and not a children's school. Those that were there are men that supported the biggest economic power in the world. They have to review their books. We will do as they do. If they kill our women and our innocent people, we will kill their women and their innocent people until they stop.

Q: Media organizations as well as intelligence information says that you run a big network in some 40 to 50 countries. There is information that al Qaeda is very influential and powerful and it is behind attacks and Islamic foundations and terrorist organizations. How much is al Qaeda dependent on Osama Bin Laden?

BIN LADEN: This has nothing to do with this poor servant of God, nor with the al Qaeda organization. We are the children of an Islamic nation whose leader is Mohammed.

We have one religion, one God, one book, one prophet, one nation. Our book teaches us to be brothers of a faith. All the Muslims are brothers. The name "al Qaeda" was established a long time ago by mere chance. The late Abu Ebeida El-Banashiri established the training camps for our mujahedeen against Russia's terrorism. We used to call the training camp al Qaeda [meaning "the base" in English]. And the name stayed. We speak about the conscience of the nation; we are the sons of the nation. We brothers in Islam from the Middle East, Philippines, Malaysia, India, Pakistan and as far as Mauritania.

Those men who sacrificed themselves in New York and Washington, they are the spokesmen of the nation's conscience. They are the nation's conscience that saw they have to avenge against the oppression.

Not all terrorism is cursed; some terrorism is blessed. A thief, a criminal, for example feels terrorized by the police. So, do we say to the policeman, "You are a terrorist"? No. Police terrorism against criminals is a blessed terrorism because it will prevent the criminal from repeating his deed. America and Israel exercise the condemned terrorism. We practice the good terrorism which stops them from killing our children in Palestine and elsewhere.

Q: What's al Qaeda's strategic plan in the Arab world. Some countries had commented about what's going on while others supported the Americans in their position toward you. The Saudi interior minister warned people against you, and against what you say, and against what you do and the path you follow. What's your reaction to his statement?

BIN LADEN: We are a part of that nation. We work hard to lift it out of oppression, and to stop those who want to manipulate its book and its God. I heard some of what the Saudi interior minister said when he said that we are turning Muslims to atheists, God forbid. Our goal is for our nation to unite in the face of the Christian crusade. This is the fiercest battle. Muslims have never faced anything bigger than this. Bush said it in his own words: "crusade." When Bush says that, they try to cover up for him, then he said he didn't mean it. He said "crusade." Bush divided the world into two: "either with us or with terrorism." Bush is the leader; he carries the big cross and walks. I swear that every one who follows Bush in his scheme has given up Islam and the word of the prophet. This is very clear. The prophet has said, "Believers don't follow Jews or Christians." Our wise people have said that those who follow the unfaithful have become unfaithful themselves. Those who follow Bush in his crusade against Muslims have denounced God.

[Bin Laden recites verses from the Quran on same subject.]

Those who support Bush, even with one word, have fallen.

Q: Even with one word: You are putting a big group of Muslims in the circle.

BIN LADEN: Know the truth and its roots. The book of God is our guide. Either Islam or atheism.

Q: Can small countries like Qatar, or Bahrain or Kuwait, which don't have much control, be excused? The Qatari foreign minister said, "I am surrounded by superpowers that will very easily wipe me off the map. That's why I have to ally myself with Americans and others."

BIN LADEN: In the subject of Islam and the killing of the faithful, what those people are doing cannot be excused. If the emir of Qatar orders someone to kill your child, and you ask this person why he did it, he'll say, "Look, brother Tayseer, I like you very much, but I was forced to do it." Nothing will excuse him for aiding the tyrant to kill your child. Your child's blood goes to waste like this. They claim that they don't have much control. Their claim that they were forced into it is not considered righteous in Islam. People's blood is being wasted in this case.

Q: What do you think of the so-called "war of civilizations"? You always keep repeating "crusaders" and words like that all the time. Does that mean you support the war of civilizations?

BIN LADEN: No doubt about that: The book mentions this clearly. The Jews and the Americans made up this call for peace in the world. The peace they're calling for is a big fairy tale. They're just drugging the Muslims as they lead them to slaughter. And the slaughter is still going on. If we defend ourselves, they call us terrorists. The prophet has said, "The end won't come before the Muslims and the Jews fight each other till the Jew hides between a tree and a stone. Then the tree and stone say, "Oh, you Muslim, this is a Jew hiding behind me. Come and kill him." He who claims there will be a lasting peace between us and the Jews is an infidel. He'll be denouncing the book and what's in it. Begin, the leader of the massacre of Kfar Yassin, and the traitor, Anwar Sadat, who sold the land and the blood of the mujahedeen both were given the Nobel Peace Prize. There will come some deceiving times where the liars will be believed and the truthful won't be believed. That's the situation in the Arabic world with its great leadership. They are lying to people. But god's relief and victory is coming soon.

Q: As you call it, this is a war between the crusaders and Muslims. How do you see the way out of this crisis?

BIN LADEN: We are in a decisive battle with the Jews and those who support them from the crusaders and the Zionists. We won't hesitate to kill the Israelis who occupied our land and kill our children and women day and night. And every person who will side with them should blame themselves only. Now how we will get out of the tunnel, that is the [unintelligible] of the other side. We were attacked, and our duty is to remove this attack. As far as the Jews are concerned, the prophet has announced that we will fight them under this name, on this land. America forced itself and its people in this [unintelligible] more than 53 years ago. It recognized Israel and supported its creation financially. In 1973, under Nixon, it supported Israel with men, weapons and ammunition from Washington all the way to Tel Aviv. This support helped change the course of history. It is the Muslim's duty to fight. ...

[America] made hilarious claims. They said that Osama's messages have codes in them to the terrorists. It's as if we were living in the time of mail by carrier pigeon, when there are no phones, no travelers, no Internet, no regular mail, no express mail, and no electronic mail. I mean, these are very humorous things. They discount people's intellects.

We swore that America wouldn't live in security until we live it truly in Palestine. This showed the reality of America, which puts Israel's interest above its own people's interest. America won't get out of this crisis until it gets out of the Arabian Peninsula, and until it stops its support of Israel. This equation can be understood by any American child, but Bush, because he's an Israeli agent, cannot understand this equation unless the swords threatened him above him head.

Q: Do you have anything to do with anthrax that is spreading around the world?

BIN LADEN: These diseases are a punishment from God and a response to oppressed mothers' prayers in Lebanon, Iraq and Palestine. There is no wall between the prayer of the oppressed and God. This is God's response to these prayers.

Q: Do you have a message for the viewers of Al-Jazeera? You know Al-Jazeera is now translated into so many languages and transmitted around the world.

BIN LADEN: In this fighting between Islam and the crusaders, we will continue our jihad. We will incite the nation for Jihad until we meet God and get his blessing. Any country that supports the Jews can only blame itself. If Sheik Suleiman Abu Gheith spoke specifically about America and Britain, this is only an example to give other countries the chance to review their books.

What do Japan or Australia or Germany have to do with this war? They just support the infidels and the crusaders.

This is a recurring war. The original crusade brought Richard [the Lionhearted] from Britain, Louis from France, and Barbarus from Germany. Today the crusading countries rushed as soon as Bush raised the cross. They accepted the rule of the cross.

What do the Arab countries have to do with this crusade? Everyone that supports Bush, even with one word, is an act of great treason. You change your name and you help the enemy to kill our children, and you are telling me we are facilitating things between us and the Americans. What are they talking about? Those who talk about the loss of innocent people didn't yet taste how it feels when you lose a child, don't know how it feels when you look in your child's eyes and all you see is fear, don't know how it feels when, in Palestine, our brothers are being hunted by army helicopters in the middle of their own homes with their families and children. Everyday. They show you the injured and the dead, and they shed tears, but no tears are shed for our women and children killed in Palestine. Are they not afraid that one day they get the same treatment?

[Bin Laden recites verses from the Quran on same subject.]

The Europeans are free, but when they side with the Jews, that their [unintelligible]. I tell Muslims to believe in the victory of God and in Jihad against the infidels of the world. The killing of Jews and Americans is one of the greatest duties.

[More Quranic verses.]

Remember the saying, "If they want to exile you, they can't exile you unless it is written by God." Don't ask anyone's opinion when it comes to the killing of Americans, and remember your appointment with God and the best of the prophets.

[More Quranic verses.]

As far as Pakistan siding with the crusaders, our brothers in Pakistan and their actions will facilitate our attack on the coalition of crusaders. Everyone supporting America, even medically, is considered renouncing Islam. Our brother in Pakistan should react pretty quick and strong in order to praise God and his prophet. Today, Islam is calling on you to act quickly.

[Quoting the farewell speech of Mohammed] "Oh, Islam, oh, Islam, there is no other god than God, and Mohammed is the prophet of God.""

October 6, 2002. Bin Laden: "Evil brings evil"[74]

"I want to explain to the American people why we attacked New York and Washington,"

"I'm inviting you to understand the message of my attack against New York and D.C., which came as an answer to your crimes."

"Evil brings evil."

"If we follow the act of these criminal bandits at the White House, the Jewish agents who are preparing to attack the Islamic world and dividing it up, without you opposing them, one would think that you don't understand the attacks at all."

"That's why I tell you, as God is my witness, whether America increases or reduces tensions, we will surely answer back in the same manner, with God's blessing and grace, and I promise you that the Islamic youth are preparing for you what will fill your hearts with horror, and they will target the centers of your economy until you stop your tyranny and terror, until one of us dies.

"We ask God to give us help."

Al-Qaeda Carefully Selected
Strategic Communication Audiences

As discussed early in this work, a key factor in determining the success of a strategic communication plan is carefully selecting the audience. A solid strategic communication plan will address both the friends and potential enemies in a particular conflict. A perfect strategic communication plan will also include messages to those neutral parties ("Fence Sitters") who can be influenced to sway for or against the strategist. And that is exactly what we see in the al-Qaeda strategic communication plan.

Five key Usama bin Laden messages (addressing focused audiences) are categorized below and are included in their entirety by category:

1. Enemies: The United States (and a separate, pre-election message to the United States) and allies of the United States;
2. Neutral ("Fence Sitters"): Iraq and Europe;
3. Divided Nation: Afghanistan (this country was split between the Taliban and those who didn't support the Taliban, but rather desired their own democracy.);
4. Friends: Islamic radicals supportive of jihad.

Enemies
November 24, 2002. Letter to America.[75]

"In the Name of Allah, the Most Gracious, the Most Merciful,

"Permission to fight (against disbelievers) is given to those (believers) who are fought against, because they have been wronged and surely, Allah is Able to give them (believers) victory" [Quran 22:39]

"Those who believe, fight in the Cause of Allah, and those who disbelieve, fight in the cause of Taghut (anything worshipped other than Allah e.g. Satan). So fight you against the friends of Satan; ever feeble is indeed the plot of Satan."[Quran 4:76]

Some American writers have published articles under the title 'On what basis are we fighting?' These articles have generated a number of responses, some of which adhered to the truth and were based on Islamic Law, and others which have not. Here we wanted to outline the truth - as an explanation and warning - hoping for Allah's reward, seeking success and support from Him.

While seeking Allah's help, we form our reply based on two questions directed at the Americans:

(Q1) Why are we fighting and opposing you?
(Q2) What are we calling you to, and what do we want from you?

As for the first question: Why are we fighting and opposing you? The answer is very simple:

(1) Because you attacked us and continue to attack us.
  a) You attacked us in Palestine:
    (i) Palestine, which has sunk under military occupation for more than 80 years. The British handed over Palestine, with your help and your support, to the Jews, who have occupied it for more than 50 years; years overflowing with oppression, tyranny, crimes, killing, expulsion, destruction and devastation. The creation and continuation of Israel is one of the greatest crimes, and you are the leaders of its criminals. And of course there is no need to explain and prove the degree of American support for Israel. The

creation of Israel is a crime which must be erased. Each and every person whose hands have become polluted in the contribution towards this crime must pay its*price, and pay for it heavily.

(ii) It brings us both laughter and tears to see that you have not yet tired of repeating your fabricated lies that the Jews have a historical right to Palestine, as it was promised to them in the Torah. Anyone who disputes with them on this alleged fact is accused of anti-semitism. This is one of the most fallacious, widely-circulated fabrications in history. The people of Palestine are pure Arabs and original Semites. It is the Muslims who are the inheritors of Moses (peace be upon him) and the inheritors of the real Torah that has not been changed. Muslims believe in all of the Prophets, including Abraham, Moses, Jesus and Muhammad, peace and blessings of Allah be upon them all. If the followers of Moses have been promised a right to Palestine in the Torah, then the Muslims are the most worthy nation of this.

When the Muslims conquered Palestine and drove out the Romans, Palestine and Jerusalem returned to Islaam, the religion of all the Prophets peace be upon them. Therefore, the call to a historical right to Palestine cannot be raised against the Islamic Ummah that believes in all the Prophets of Allah (peace and blessings be upon them) - and we make no distinction between them.

(iii) The blood pouring out of Palestine must be equally revenged. You must know that the Palestinians do not cry alone; their women are not widowed alone; their sons are not orphaned alone.

(b) You attacked us in Somalia; you supported the Russian atrocities against us in Chechnya, the Indian oppression against us in Kashmir, and the Jewish aggression against us in Lebanon.

(c) Under your supervision, consent and orders, the governments of our countries which act as your agents, attack us on a daily basis;

(i) These governments prevent our people from establishing the Islamic Shariah, using violence and lies to do so.

(ii) These governments give us a taste of humiliation, and places us in a large prison of fear and subdual.

(iii) These governments steal our Ummah's wealth and sell them to you at a paltry price.

(iv) These governments have surrendered to the Jews, and handed them most of Palestine, acknowledging the existence of their state over the dismembered limbs of their own people.

(v) The removal of these governments is an obligation upon us, and a necessary step to free the Ummah, to make the Shariah the supreme law and to regain Palestine. And our fight against these governments is not separate from out fight against you.

(d) You steal our wealth and oil at paltry prices because of you international influence and military threats. This theft is indeed the biggest theft ever witnessed by mankind in the history of the world.

(e) Your forces occupy our countries; you spread your military bases throughout them; you corrupt our lands, and you besiege our sanctities, to protect the security of the Jews and to ensure the continuity of your pillage of our treasures.

(f) You have starved the Muslims of Iraq, where children die every day. It is a wonder that more than 1.5 million Iraqi children have died as a result of your sanctions, and you did not show concern. Yet when 3000 of your people died, the entire world rises and has not yet sat down.

(g) You have supported the Jews in their idea that Jerusalem is their eternal capital, and agreed to move your embassy there. With your help and under your protection, the Israelis are planning to destroy the Al-Aqsa mosque. Under the protection of your weapons, Sharon entered the Al-Aqsa mosque, to pollute it as a preparation to capture and destroy it.

(2) These tragedies and calamities are only a few examples of your oppression and aggression against us. It is commanded by our religion and intellect that the oppressed have a right to return the aggression. Do not await anything from us but Jihad, resistance and revenge. Is it in any way rational to expect that after America has attacked us for more than half a century, that we will then leave her to live in security and peace?!!

(3) You may then dispute that all the above does not justify aggression against civilians, for crimes they did not commit and offenses in which they did not partake:

(a) This argument contradicts your continuous repetition that America is the land of freedom, and its leaders in this world. Therefore, the American people are the ones who choose their government by way of their own free will; a choice which stems from their agreement to its policies. Thus the American people have chosen, consented to, and affirmed their support for the Israeli oppression of the Palestinians, the occupation and usurpation of their land, and its continuous killing, torture, punishment and expulsion of the Palestinians. The American people have the ability and choice to refuse the policies of their Government and even to change it if they want.

(b) The American people are the ones who pay the taxes which fund the planes that bomb us in Afghanistan, the tanks that strike and destroy our homes in Palestine, the armies which occupy our lands in the Arabian Gulf, and the fleets which ensure the blockade of Iraq. These tax dollars are given to Israel for it to continue to attack us and penetrate our lands. So the American people are the ones who fund the attacks against us, and they are the ones who oversee the expenditure of these monies in the way they wish, through their elected candidates.

(c) Also the American army is part of the American people. It is this very same people who are shamelessly helping the Jews fight against us.

(d) The American people are the ones who employ both their men and their women in the American Forces which attack us.

(e) This is why the American people cannot be not innocent of all the crimes committed by the Americans and Jews against us.

(f) Allah, the Almighty, legislated the permission and the option to take revenge. Thus, if we are attacked, then we have the right to attack back. Whoever has destroyed our villages and towns, then we have the right to destroy their villages and towns. Whoever has stolen our wealth, then we have the right to destroy their economy. And whoever has killed our civilians, then we have the right to kill theirs.

The American Government and press still refuses to answer the question: Why did they attack us in New York and Washington?

If Sharon is a man of peace in the eyes of Bush, then we are also men of peace!!! America does not understand the language of manners and principles, so we are addressing it using the language it understands.

(Q2) As for the second question that we want to answer: What are we calling you to, and what do we want from you?

(1) The first thing that we are calling you to is Islam.

(a) The religion of the Unification of God; of freedom from associating partners with Him, and rejection of this; of complete love of Him, the Exalted; of complete submission to His Laws; and of the discarding of all the opinions, orders, theories and religions which contradict with the religion He sent down to His Prophet Muhammad (peace be upon him). Islam is the religion of all the prophets, and makes no distinction between them - peace be upon them all.

It is to this religion that we call you; the seal of all the previous religions. It is the religion of Unification of God, sincerity, the best of manners, righteousness, mercy, honour, purity, and piety. It is the religion of showing kindness to others, establishing justice between them, granting them their rights, and defending the oppressed and the persecuted. It is the religion of enjoining the good and forbidding the evil with the hand, tongue and heart. It is the religion of Jihad in the way of Allah so that Allah's Word and religion reign Supreme. And it is the religion of unity and agreement on the obedience to Allah, and total equality between all people, without regarding their colour, sex, or language.

(b) It is the religion whose book - the Quran - will remained preserved and unchanged, after the other Divine books and messages have been changed. The Quran is the miracle until the

Day of Judgment. Allah has challenged anyone to bring a book like the Quran or even ten verses like it.

(2) The second thing we call you to, is to stop your oppression, lies, immorality and debauchery that has spread among you.

(a) We call you to be a people of manners, principles, honour, and purity; to reject the immoral acts of fornication, homosexuality, intoxicants, gambling's, and trading with interest.

We call you to all of this that you may be freed from that which you have become caught up in; that you may be freed from the deceptive lies that you are a great nation, that your leaders spread amongst you to conceal from you the despicable state to which you have reached.

(b) It is saddening to tell you that you are the worst civilization witnessed by the history of mankind:

(i) You are the nation who, rather than ruling by the Shariah of Allah in its Constitution and Laws, choose to invent your own laws as you will and desire. You separate religion from your policies, contradicting the pure nature which affirms Absolute Authority to the Lord and your Creator. You flee from the embarrassing question posed to you: How is it possible for Allah the Almighty to create His creation, grant them power over all the creatures and land, grant them all the amenities of life, and then deny them that which they are most in need of: knowledge of the laws which govern their lives?

(ii) You are the nation that permits Usury, which has been forbidden by all the religions. Yet you build your economy and investments on Usury. As a result of this, in all its different forms and guises, the Jews have taken control of your economy, through which they have then taken control of your media, and now control all aspects of your life making you their servants and achieving their aims at your expense; precisely what Benjamin Franklin warned you against.

(iii) You are a nation that permits the production, trading and usage of intoxicants. You also permit drugs, and only forbid the trade of them, even though your nation is the largest consumer of them.

(iv) You are a nation that permits acts of immorality, and you consider them to be pillars of personal freedom. You have continued to sink down this abyss from level to level until incest has spread amongst you, in the face of which neither your sense of honour nor your laws object.

Who can forget your President Clinton's immoral acts committed in the official Oval office? After that you did not even bring him to account, other than that he 'made a mistake', after which everything passed with no punishment. Is there a worse kind of event for which your name will go down in history and remembered by nations?

(v) You are a nation that permits gambling in its all forms. The companies practice this as well, resulting in the investments becoming active and the criminals becoming rich.

(vi) You are a nation that exploits women like consumer products or advertising tools calling upon customers to purchase them. You use women to serve passengers, visitors, and strangers to increase your profit margins. You then rant that you support the liberation of women.

(vii) You are a nation that practices the trade of sex in all its forms, directly and indirectly. Giant corporations and establishments are established on this, under the name of art, entertainment, tourism and freedom, and other deceptive names you attribute to it.

(viii) And because of all this, you have been described in history as a nation that spreads diseases that were unknown to man in the past. Go ahead and boast to the nations of man, that you brought them AIDS as a Satanic American Invention.

(xi) You have destroyed nature with your industrial waste and gases more than any other nation in history. Despite this, you refuse to sign the Kyoto agreement so that you can secure the profit of your greedy companies and*industries.

(x) Your law is the law of the rich and wealthy people, who hold sway in their political parties, and fund their election campaigns with their gifts. Behind them stand the Jews, who control your policies, media and economy.

(xi) That which you are singled out for in the history of mankind, is that you have used your force to destroy mankind more than any other nation in history; not to defend principles and values, but to hasten to secure your interests and profits. You who dropped a nuclear bomb on Japan, even though Japan was ready to negotiate an end to the war. How many acts of oppression, tyranny and injustice have you carried out, O callers to freedom?

(xii) Let us not forget one of your major characteristics: your duality in both manners and values; your hypocrisy in manners and principles. All*manners, principles and values have two scales: one for you and one for the others.

(a)The freedom and democracy that you call to is for yourselves and for white race only; as for the rest of the world, you impose upon them your monstrous, destructive policies and

Governments, which you call the 'American friends'. Yet you prevent them from establishing democracies. When the Islamic party in Algeria wanted to practice democracy and they won the election, you unleashed your agents in the Algerian army onto them, and to attack them with tanks and guns, to imprison them and torture them - a new lesson from the 'American book of democracy'!!!

(b) Your policy on prohibiting and forcibly removing weapons of mass destruction to ensure world peace: it only applies to those countries which you do not permit to possess such weapons. As for the countries you consent to, such as Israel, then they are allowed to keep and use such weapons to defend their security. Anyone else who you suspect might be manufacturing or keeping these kinds of weapons, you call them criminals and you take military action against them.

(c) You are the last ones to respect the resolutions and policies of International Law, yet you claim to want to selectively punish anyone else who does the same. Israel has for more than 50 years been pushing UN resolutions and rules against the wall with the full support of America.

(d) As for the war criminals which you censure and form criminal courts for - you shamelessly ask that your own are granted immunity!! However, history will not forget the war crimes that you committed against the Muslims and the rest of the world; those you have killed in Japan, Afghanistan, Somalia, Lebanon and Iraq will remain a shame that you will never be able to escape. It will suffice to remind you of your latest war crimes in Afghanistan, in which densely populated innocent civilian villages were destroyed, bombs were dropped on mosques causing the roof of the mosque to come crashing down on the heads of the Muslims praying inside. You are the ones who broke the agreement with the Mujahideen when they left Qunduz, bombing them in Jangi fort, and killing more than 1,000 of your prisoners through suffocation and thirst. Allah alone knows how many people have died by torture at the hands of you and your agents. Your planes remain in the Afghan skies, looking for anyone remotely suspicious.

(e) You have claimed to be the vanguards of Human Rights, and your Ministry of Foreign affairs issues annual reports containing statistics of those countries that violate any Human Rights. However, all these things vanished when the Mujahideen hit you, and you then implemented the methods of the same documented governments that you used to curse. In America, you captured thousands the Muslims and Arabs, took them into custody with neither reason, court trial, nor even disclosing their names. You issued newer, harsher laws.

What happens in Guatanamo is a historical embarrassment to America and its values, and it screams into your faces - you hypocrites, "What is the value of your signature on any agreement or treaty?"

(3) What we call you to thirdly is to take an honest stance with yourselves - and I doubt you will do so - to discover that you are a nation without principles or manners, and that the values and principles to you are something which you merely demand from others, not that which you yourself must adhere to.

(4) We also advise you to stop supporting Israel, and to end your support of the Indians in Kashmir, the Russians against the Chechens and to also cease supporting the Manila Government against the Muslims in Southern Philippines.

(5) We also advise you to pack your luggage and get out of our lands. We desire for your goodness, guidance, and righteousness, so do not force us to send you back as cargo in coffins.

(6) Sixthly, we call upon you to end your support of the corrupt leaders in our countries. Do not interfere in our politics and method of education. Leave us alone, or else expect us in New York and Washington.

(7) We also call you to deal with us and interact with us on the basis of mutual interests and benefits, rather than the policies of sub dual, theft and occupation, and not to continue your policy of supporting the Jews because this will result in more disasters for you.

If you fail to respond to all these conditions, then prepare for fight with the Islamic Nation. The Nation of Monotheism, that puts complete trust on Allah and fears none other than Him. The Nation which is addressed by its Quran with the words: "Do you fear them? Allah has more right that you should fear Him if you are believers. Fight against them so that Allah will punish them by your hands and disgrace them and give you victory over them and heal the breasts of believing people. And remove the anger of their (believers') hearts. Allah accepts the repentance of whom He wills. Allah is All-Knowing, All-Wise." [Quran9:13-1]

The Nation of honour and respect:

"But honour, power and glory belong to Allah, and to His Messenger (Muhammad- peace be upon him) and to the believers." [Quran 63:8]

"So do not become weak (against your enemy), nor be sad, and you will be*superior (in victory)if you are indeed (true) believers" [Quran 3:139]

The Nation of Martyrdom; the Nation that desires death more than you desire life:

"Think not of those who are killed in the way of Allah as dead. Nay, they are alive with their Lord, and they are being provided for. They rejoice in what Allah has bestowed upon them from His bounty and rejoice for the sake of those who have not yet joined them, but are left behind (not yet martyred) that on them no fear shall come, nor shall they grieve. They rejoice in a grace and a bounty from Allah, and that Allah will not waste the reward of the believers." [Quran 3:169-171]

The Nation of victory and success that Allah has promised:

"It is He Who has sent His Messenger (Muhammad peace be upon him) with guidance and the religion of truth (Islam), to make it victorious over all other religions even though the Polytheists hate it." [Quran 61:9]

"Allah has decreed that 'Verily it is I and My Messengers who shall be victorious.' Verily Allah is All-Powerful, All-Mighty." [Quran 58:21]

The Islamic Nation that was able to dismiss and destroy the previous evil Empires like yourself; the Nation that rejects your attacks, wishes to remove your evils, and is prepared to fight you. You are well aware that the Islamic Nation, from the very core of its soul, despises your haughtiness and arrogance.

If the Americans refuse to listen to our advice and the goodness, guidance and righteousness that we call them to, then be aware that you will lose this Crusade Bush began, just like the other previous Crusades in which you were humiliated by the hands of the Mujahideen, fleeing to your home in great silence and disgrace. If the Americans do not respond, then their fate will be that of the Soviets who fled from Afghanistan to deal with their military defeat, political breakup, ideological downfall, and economic bankruptcy.

This is our message to the Americans, as an answer to theirs. Do they now know why we fight them and over which form of ignorance, by the permission of Allah, we shall be victorious?"

October 29, 2004. A message to Pre-Midterm Election America.[76]

"O American people, I address these words to you regarding the best way of avoiding another Manhattan, and regarding the war, its causes and its consequences. But before this, I say to you: Security is one of the important pillars of human life, and free men do not take their security lightly, contrary to Bush's claim that we hate freedom. Let him explain why we did not attack Sweden, for example. Clearly, those who hate freedom – unlike the 19, may Allah have mercy on them – have no self-esteem. We have been fighting you because we are free men who do not remain silent in the face of injustice. We want to restore our [Islamic] nation's freedom. Just as you violate our security, we violate yours. Whoever toys with the security of others, deluding himself that he will remain secure, is nothing but a foolish thief. One of the most important things rational people do when calamities occur is to look for their causes so as to avoid them.

"But I am amazed at you. Although we have entered the fourth year after the events of 9/11, Bush is still practicing distortion and deception against you and he is still concealing the true cause from you. Consequentially, the motives for its reoccurrence still exist. I will tell you about the causes underlying these events and I will tell you the truth about the moments this decision was taken, to allow you to reflect.

"I say to you, as Allah is my witness: We had not considered attacking the towers, but things reached the breaking point when we witnessed the iniquity and tyranny of the American-Israeli coalition against our people in Palestine and Lebanon – then I got this idea.

"The events that had a direct influence on me occurred in 1982, and the subsequent events, when the U.S. permitted the Israelis to invade Lebanon with the aid of the American sixth fleet. They started shelling, and many were killed and wounded, while others were terrorized into fleeing. I still remember those moving scenes – blood, torn limbs, and dead women and children; ruined homes everywhere, and high-rises being demolished on top of their residents; bombs raining down mercilessly on our homes. It was as though a crocodile swallowed a child, and he could do nothing but cry. But does a crocodile understand any language other than arms? The entire world saw and heard, but did not respond.

"In those critical moments, I was overwhelmed by ideas that are hard to describe, but they awakened a powerful impulse to reject injustice and gave birth to a firm resolve to punish the oppressors. As I was looking at those destroyed towers in Lebanon, I was struck by the idea of punishing the oppressor in the same manner and destroying towers in the U.S., to give it a taste of what we have tasted and to deter it from killing our children and women. That day I became convinced that iniquity and the premeditated murder of innocent children and women is an established American principle, and that terror is [the real meaning of] 'freedom' and 'democracy,' while they call the resistance 'terrorism' and 'reaction.' America stands for iniquity and for imposing sanctions on millions of people, resulting in the death of many, as Bush Sr. did, causing the mass slaughter of children in Iraq, [the worst] that humanity has ever known. It stands for dropping millions of pounds of bombs and explosives on millions of children in Iraq again, as Bush Jr. did, in order to depose an old agent and to appoint a new agent to help him steal Iraq's oil, and other sorts of horrible things.

"It was against the backdrop of these and similar images that 9/11 came in response to these terrible iniquities. Should a man be blamed for protecting his own? And is defending oneself and punishing the wicked an eye for an eye – is that reprehensible terrorism? Even if it is reprehensible terrorism, we have no other choice. This is the message that we have tried to convey to you, in words and in deeds, more than once in the years preceding 9/11. Observe it, if you will, in the interview with Scott in Time Magazine in 1996, and with Peter Arnett on CNN in 1997, then John Wiener [?] in 1998; observe it, if you will, in the deeds of Nairobi and Tanzania and Aden, and observe it in my interview with 'Abd Al-Bari 'Atwan and in interviews with Robert Fisk. The latter is of your own and of your religious affiliation, and I consider him to be unbiased.

"Would those who claim to stand for freedom in the White House and in the TV stations that answer to them, would they conduct an interview with him [Fisk] so that he might convey to the American people what he has understood from us concerning the causes of our fight against you? For if you were to avoid these causes, you would take America in the right path to the security it knew before 9/11. So much for the war and its causes.

"As for its results, they are very positive, with Allah's grace. They surpassed all expectations by all criteria for many reasons, one of the most important of which is that we had no difficulty dealing with Bush and his administration, because it resembles the regimes in our [Arab] countries, half of which are ruled by the military, and the other half are ruled by the sons of kings and presidents with whom we have had a lot of experience. Among both types, there are many who are known for their conceit, arrogance, greed, and for taking money unrightfully.

"This resemblance began with the visit of Bush Sr. to the region. While some of our people were dazzled by the U.S. and hoped that these visits would influence our countries, it was he who was influenced by these monarchic and military regimes. He envied them for remaining in their positions for decades, while embezzling the nation's public funds with no supervision whatsoever. He bequeathed tyranny and the suppression of liberties to his son and they called it the Patriot Act, under the pretext of war on terrorism.

"Bush Sr. liked the idea of appointing his sons as state [*wilaya*] governors. Similarly, he did not neglect to import to Florida the expertise in falsifying [elections] from the leaders of this region in order to benefit from it in difficult moments.

"As previously mentioned, it was easy for us to provoke this administration and to drag it [after us]. It was enough for us to send two *Jihad* fighters to the farthest east to hoist a rag on which 'Al-Qa'ida' was written – that was enough to cause generals to rush off to this place, thereby causing America human and financial and political losses, without it accomplishing anything worthy of mention, apart from giving business to [the generals'] private corporations. Besides, we gained experience in guerilla warfare and in conducting a war of attrition in our fight with the iniquitous, great power, that is, when we conducted a war of attrition against Russia with *Jihad* fighters for 10 years until they went bankrupt, with Allah's grace; as a result, they were forced to withdraw in defeat, all praise and thanks to Allah. We are continuing in the same policy – to make America bleed profusely to the point of bankruptcy, Allah willing. And that is not too difficult for Allah.

"Whoever says that Al-Qa'ida triumphed over the White House administration, or that the White House administration lost this war – this is not entirely accurate, for if we look carefully at the results, it is impossible to say that Al-Qa'ida is the only cause for these amazing gains. The White House policy, which strove to open war fronts so as to give business to their various corporations – be they in the field of armament, of oil, or of construction – also helped in accomplishing these astonishing achievements for Al-Qa'ida. It appeared to some analysts and diplomats as though we and the White House play as one team to score a goal against the United States of America, even though our intentions differ. Such ideas, and some others, were pointed out by a British diplomat in the course of a lecture at the Royal Institute for International Affairs; for example, that Al-Qa'ida spent $500,000 on the event [9/11] while America lost in the event and its subsequent effects more than 500 billion dollars; that is to say that each of Al-Qa'ida's dollars defeated one million American dollars, thanks to Allah's grace. This is in addition to the fact that America lost a large number of jobs, and as for the [federal] deficit, it lost a record number estimated at a trillion dollars.

"Even more serious for America is the fact that the *Jihad* fighters have recently forced Bush to resort to an emergency budget in order to continue the fighting in Afghanistan and in Iraq, which proves the success of the plan of bleeding [America] to the point of bankruptcy, Allah willing.

"Indeed, all of this makes it clear that Al-Qa'ida won gains; but on the other hand, it also makes it clear that the Bush administration won gains as well, since anyone who looks at the scope of the contracts won by large dubious corporations like Halliburton and other similar ones that have ties to Bush and to his administration will become convinced that the losing side is in fact you, the American people, and your economy.

"We agreed with the general commander Muhammad Atta, may Allah have mercy on him, that all operations should be carried out within 20 minutes, before Bush and his administration would become aware. We never imagined that the Commander in Chief of the American armed forces would abandon 50,000 of his citizens in the twin towers to face this great horror alone when they needed him most. It seemed to him

JIHADIST STRATEGIC COMMUNICATION

that a girl's story about her goat and its butting was more important than dealing with planes and their 'butting' into skyscrapers. This allowed us three times the amount of time needed for the operations, Allah be praised.

"It should be no secret to you that American thinkers and intellectuals warned Bush before the war: all that you [Bush] need in order to assure America's security by ridding [Iraq] of weapons of mass destruction, assuming there were any, is at your disposal, and all the countries of the world are with you in the matter of carrying out inspections, and the U.S.'s interest does not require you to drive it into an unjustified war, whose end you cannot know.

"However, the blackness of black gold blinded his sight and his perception and he gave preference to private interests over America's public interest. And so there was war and many died. The American economy bled and Bush became embroiled in the quagmire of Iraq, which now threatens his future.

"His case is like that [described in the parable]:

"He is like the ill-tempered goat that dug out of the ground the sharp knife [with which it would be slaughtered].

"I say to you: more than 15,000 of our people were killed and tens of thousands were wounded, just as more than 1,000 of you were killed and more than 10,000 wounded, and Bush's hands are sullied with the blood of all of these casualties on both sides, for the sake of oil and to give business to his private companies. You should know that a nation that punishes a weak person if he is instrumental in killing one of that nation's sons for money, while letting go free a high-class man who was instrumental in killing more than 1,000 of its sons, also for money [sic]. Similarly your allies in Palestine intimidate women and children and murder and imprison men. [inaudible]

"Keep in mind that every action has a reaction, and finally you should consider the last wills and testaments of the thousands who left you on 9/11, waving their hands in despair. These are inspiring wills, which deserve to be published and studied thoroughly. One of the most important things I have read regarding their hand-waving signals before they fell is that they were saying 'We were wrong to let the White House carry out unchecked its aggressive foreign policy against oppressed people.' As though they were telling you, the American people, 'You should call to task those who caused our death.' Happy is he who learns a lesson from the experience of others. A verse that I have read is also relevant to their [last] signals:

"Evil kills those who perpetrate it,

"And the pastures of iniquity are harmful.

"There is a saying: a small amount spent on prevention is better than a great amount spent on treatment. You should know that it is better to return to that which is right than to persist in that which is wrong. A rational man would not neglect his security, property, or home for the sake of the liar in the White House.

"Your security is not in the hands of Kerry or Bush or Al-Qa'ida. Your security is in your own hands, and any [U.S.] state [*wilaya*] that does not toy with our security automatically guarantees its own security.

"Allah is our guardian but you have none.

"Peace be upon whoever follows the true guidance."

November 12, 2002. Letter to America's Allies.[77]

"In the name of God, the merciful, the compassionate, from the slave of God, Osama Bin Laden, to the peoples of the countries allied with the tyrannical US Government:

May God's peace be upon those who follow the right path. The road to safety begins by ending the aggression.

Reciprocal treatment is part of justice.

The incidents that have taken place since the raids on New York and Washington up until now - like the killing of Germans in Tunisia and the French in Karachi, the bombing of the giant French tanker in Yemen, the killing of marines in Failaka [in Kuwait] and the British and Australians in the Bali explosions, the recent operation in Moscow and some sporadic operations here and there - are only reactions and reciprocal actions.

These actions were carried out by the zealous sons of Islam in defence of their religion and in response to the order of their God and prophet, may God's peace and blessings be upon him.

White House 'criminals'

What [US President George] Bush, the pharaoh of this age, was doing in terms of killing our sons in Iraq, and what Israel, the United States' ally, was doing in terms of bombing houses that shelter old people, women and children with US-made aircraft in Palestine were sufficient to prompt the sane among your rulers to distance themselves from this criminal gang. Our kinfolk in Palestine have been slain and severely tortured for nearly a century.

If we defend our people in Palestine, the world becomes agitated and allies itself against Muslims, unjustly and falsely, under the pretence of fighting terrorism.

What do your governments want by allying themselves with the criminal gang in the White House against Muslims?

Do your governments not know that the White House gangsters are the biggest butchers of this age?

[US Defence Secretary Donald] Rumsfeld, the butcher of Vietnam, killed more than two million people, not to mention those he wounded.

[US Vice-President Dick] Cheney and [US Secretary of State Colin] Powell killed and destroyed in Baghdad more than Hulegu of the Mongols.

What do your governments want from their alliance with America in attacking us in Afghanistan?

I mention in particular Britain, France, Italy, Canada, Germany and Australia.

We warned Australia before not to join in [the war] in Afghanistan, and [against] its despicable effort to separate East Timor.

It ignored the warning until it woke up to the sounds of explosions in Bali.

Its government falsely claimed that they [the Australians] were not targeted.

'You will be killed'

If you were distressed by the deaths of your men and the men of your allies in Tunisia, Karachi, Failaka, Bali and Amman, remember our children who are killed in Palestine and Iraq everyday, remember our deaths in Khowst mosques and remember the premeditated killing of our people in weddings in Afghanistan.

If you were distressed by the killing of your nationals in Moscow, remember ours in Chechnya.

Why should fear, killing, destruction, displacement, orphaning and widowing continue to be our lot, while security, stability and happiness be your lot?

This is unfair. It is time that we get even. You will be killed just as you kill, and will be bombed just as you bomb.

And expect more that will further distress you. The Islamic nation, thanks to God, has started to attack you at the hands of its beloved sons, who pledged to God to continue jihad, as long as they are alive, through words and weapons to establish right and expose falsehood.

In conclusion, I ask God to help us champion His religion and continue jihad for His sake until we meet Him while He is satisfied with us. And He can do so. Praise be to Almighty God."

Neutrals

April 15, 2004. Post-Madrid Bombing: Letter to the People of Europe.[78]

"Praise be to Almighty God; Peace and prayers be upon our Prophet Muhammad, his family, and companions.

This is a message to our neighbours north of the Mediterranean, containing a reconciliation initiative as a response to their positive reactions.

Praise be to God; praise be to God; praise be to God who created heaven and earth with justice and who allowed the oppressed to punish the oppressor in the same way.

Peace upon those who followed the right path:

'Oppression kills the oppressors'

In my hands there is a message to remind you that justice is a duty towards those whom you love and those whom you do not. And people's rights will not be harmed if the opponent speaks out about them.

The greatest rule of safety is justice, and stopping injustice and aggression. It was said: Oppression kills the oppressors and the hotbed of injustice is evil. The situation in occupied Palestine is an example. What happened on 11 September [2001] and 11 March [the Madrid train bombings] is your commodity that was returned to you.

It is known that security is a pressing necessity for all mankind. We do not agree that you should monopolise it only for yourselves. Also, vigilant people do not allow their politicians to tamper with their security.

Having said this, we would like to inform you that labelling us and our acts as terrorism is also a description of you and of your acts. Reaction comes at the same level as the original action. Our acts are reaction to your own acts, which are represented by the destruction and killing of our kinfolk in Afghanistan, Iraq and Palestine.

The act that horrified the world; that is, the killing of the old, handicapped [Hamas spiritual leader] Sheikh Ahmed Yassin, may God have mercy on him, is sufficient evidence.

We pledge to God that we will punish America for him, God willing.

Which religion considers your killed ones innocent and our killed ones worthless? And which principle considers your blood real blood and our blood water? Reciprocal treatment is fair and the one who starts injustice bears greater blame.

'Bloodsuckers'

As for your politicians and those who have followed their path, who insist on ignoring the real problem of occupying the entirety of Palestine and exaggerate lies and falsification regarding our right in defence and resistance, they do not respect themselves.

They also disdain the blood and minds of peoples. This is because their falsification increases the shedding of your blood instead of sparing it.

Moreover, the examining of the developments that have been taking place, in terms of killings in our countries and your countries, will make clear an important fact; namely, that injustice is inflicted on us and on you by your politicians, who send your sons - although you are opposed to this - to our countries to kill and be killed.

Therefore, it is in both sides' interest to curb the plans of those who shed the blood of peoples for their narrow personal interest and subservience to the White House gang.

We must take into consideration that this war brings billions of dollars in profit to the major companies, whether it be those that produce weapons or those that contribute to reconstruction, such as the Halliburton Company, its sisters and daughters.

Based on this, it is very clear who is the one benefiting from igniting this war and from the shedding of blood. It is the warlords, the bloodsuckers, who are steering the world policy from behind a curtain.

As for President Bush, the leaders who are revolving in his orbit, the leading media companies and the United Nations, which makes laws for relations between the masters of veto and the slaves of the General Assembly, these are only some of the tools used to deceive and exploit peoples.

All these pose a fatal threat to the whole world.

The Zionist lobby is one of the most dangerous and most difficult figures of this group. God willing, we are determined to fight them.

'Reconciliation initiative'

Based on the above, and in order to deny war merchants a chance and in response to the positive interaction shown by recent events and opinion polls, which indicate that most European peoples want peace, I ask honest people, especially ulema, preachers and merchants, to form a permanent committee to enlighten European peoples of the justice of our causes, above all Palestine. They can make use of the huge potential of the media.

I also offer a reconciliation initiative to them, whose essence is our commitment to stopping operations against every country that commits itself to not attacking Muslims or interfering in their affairs - including the US conspiracy on the greater Muslim world.

This reconciliation can be renewed once the period signed by the first government expires and a second government is formed with the consent of both parties.

The reconciliation will start with the departure of its last soldier from our country.

The door of reconciliation is open for three months of the date of announcing this statement.

For those who reject reconciliation and want war, we are ready.

As for those who want reconciliation, we have given them a chance. Stop shedding our blood so as to preserve your blood. It is in your hands to apply this easy, yet difficult, formula. You know that the situation will expand and increase if you delay things.

If this happens, do not blame us - blame yourselves.

A rational person does not relinquish his security, money and children to please the liar of the White House.

Had he been truthful about his claim for peace, he would not describe the person who ripped open pregnant women in Sabra and Shatila [reference to Israeli Prime Minister Ariel Sharon] and the destroyer of the capitulation process [reference to the Palestinian-Israeli peace process] as a man of peace.

He also would not have lied to people and said that we hate freedom and kill for the sake of killing. Reality proves our truthfulness and his lie.

The killing of the Russians was after their invasion of Afghanistan and Chechnya; the killing of Europeans was after their invasion of Iraq and Afghanistan; and the killing of Americans on the day of New

York [reference to 11 September] was after their support of the Jews in Palestine and their invasion of the Arabian Peninsula.

Also, killing them in Somalia was after their invasion of it in Operation Restore Hope. We made them leave without hope, praise be to God.

It is said that prevention is better than cure. A happy person is he who learns a lesson from the experience of others.

Heeding right is better than persisting in falsehood.

Peace be upon those who follow guidance."

February 11, 2003. Message to the Muslim People in Iraq.[79]

"In the name of God, the merciful, the compassionate.

A message to our Muslim brothers in Iraq, may God's peace, mercy, and blessings be upon you.

O you who believe fear Allah, by doing all that He has ordered and by abstaining from all that He has forbidden as He should be feared.

Obey Him, be thankful to Him, and remember Him always, and die not except in a state of Islam [as Muslims] with complete submission to Allah.

We are following up with great interest and extreme concern the crusaders' preparations for war to occupy a former capital of Islam, loot Muslims' wealth, and install an agent government, which would be a satellite for its masters in Washington and Tel Aviv, just like all the other treasonous and agent Arab governments.

This would be in preparation for establishing the Greater Israel.

Allah is sufficient for us and He is the best disposer of affairs.

'Unjust war'

Amid this unjust war, the war of infidels and debauchees led by America along with its allies and agents, we would like to stress a number of important values:

First, showing good intentions. This means fighting should be for the sake of the one God.

It should not be for championing ethnic groups, or for championing the non-Islamic regimes in all Arab countries, including Iraq.

God Almighty says: "Those who believe fight in the cause of Allah, and those who reject faith fight in the cause of evil."

So fight ye against the friends of Satan: feeble indeed is the cunning of Satan.

Second, we remind that victory comes only from God and all we have to do is prepare and motivate for jihad.

God Almighty says: "Oh ye who believe! If ye will help the cause of Allah, He will help you and plant your feet firmly."

We must rush to seek God Almighty's forgiveness from sins, particularly the grave sins.

Prophet Muhammad, God's peace be upon him, said: "Avoid the seven grave sins; polytheism, sorcery, killing, unless permitted by God, usury, taking the money of orphans, fleeing from combat, and slandering innocent faithful women."

Also, all grave sins, such as consuming alcohol, committing adultery, disobeying parents, and committing perjury. We must obey God in general, and should in particular mention the name of God more before combat.

'Media machine'

Abu-al-Darda, may God be pleased with him, said: "Perform a good deed before an attack, because you are fighting with your deeds."

Third, we realized from our defence and fighting against the American enemy that, in combat, they mainly depend on psychological warfare.

This is in light of the huge media machine they have.

They also depend on massive air strikes so as to conceal their most prominent point of weakness, which is the fear, cowardliness, and the absence of combat spirit among US soldiers.

Those soldiers are completely convinced of the injustice and lying of their government.

They also lack a fair cause to defend. They only fight for capitalists, usury takers, and the merchants of arms and oil, including the gang of crime at the White House.

This is in addition to crusader and personal grudges by Bush the father.

Trench warfare

We also realized that one of the most effective and available methods of rendering the air force of the crusader enemy ineffective is by setting up roofed and disguised trenches in large numbers.

I had referred to that in a previous statement during the Tora Bora battle last year.

In that great battle, faith triumphed over all the materialistic forces of the people of evil, for principles were adhered to, thanks to God Almighty.

I will narrate to you part of that great battle, to show how cowardly they are on the one hand, and how effective trenches are in exhausting them on the other.

We were about 300 mujahideen [Islamic militants].We dug 100 trenches that were spread in an area that does not exceed one square mile, one trench for every three brothers, so as to avoid the huge human losses resulting from the bombardment.

Since the first hour of the US campaign on 20 Rajab 1422, corresponding to 7 October 2001, our centres were exposed to a concentrated bombardment.

And this bombardment continued until mid-Ramadan.

On 17 Ramadan, a very fierce bombardment began, particularly after the US command was certain that some of al-Qaeda leaders were still in Tora Bora, including the humble servant to God [referring to himself] and the brother mujahid Dr Ayman al-Zawahiri.

The bombardment was round-the-clock and the warplanes continued to fly over us day and night.

War in Afghanistan

The US Pentagon, together with its allies, worked full time on blowing up and destroying this small spot, as well as on removing it entirely.

Planes poured their lava on us, particularly after accomplishing their main missions in Afghanistan.

The US forces attacked us with smart bombs, bombs that weigh thousands of pounds, cluster bombs, and bunker busters.

Bombers, like the B-52, used to fly over head for more than two hours and drop between 20 to 30 bombs at a time.

The modified C-130 aircraft kept carpet-bombing us at night, using modern types of bombs.

The US forces dared not break into our positions, despite the unprecedented massive bombing and terrible propaganda targeting this completely besieged small area.

This is in addition to the forces of hypocrites, whom they prodded to fight us for 15 days non-stop.

Every time the latter attacked us, we forced them out of our area carrying their dead and wounded.

'Alliance of evil'

Is there any clearer evidence of their cowardice, fear, and lies regarding their legends about their alleged power.

To sum it up, the battle resulted in the complete failure of the international alliance of evil, with all its forces, [to overcome] a small number of mujahideen - 300 mujahideen hunkered down in trenches spread over an area of one square mile under a temperature of -10 degrees Celsius.

The battle resulted in the injury of 6% of personnel - we hope God will accept them as martyrs - and the damage of two percent of the trenches, praise be to God.

If all the world forces of evil could not achieve their goals on a one square mile of area against a small number of mujahideen with very limited capabilities, how can these evil forces triumph over the Muslim world?

This is impossible, God willing, if people adhere to their religion and insist on jihad for its sake.

Iraqi 'brothers'

O mujahideen brothers in Iraq, do not be afraid of what the United States is propagating in terms of their lies about their power and their smart, laser-guided missiles.

The smart bombs will have no effect worth mentioning in the hills and in the trenches, on plains, and in forests.

They must have apparent targets. The well-camouflaged trenches and targets will not be reached by either the smart or the stupid missiles.

There will only be haphazard strikes that dissipate the enemy ammunition and waste its money. Dig many trenches.

The [early Muslim caliph] Umar, may God be pleased with him, stated: "Take the ground as a shield because this will ensure the exhaustion of all the stored enemy missiles within months."

Their daily production is too little and can be dealt with, God willing.

We also recommend luring the enemy forces into a protracted, close, and exhausting fight, using the camouflaged defensive positions in plains, farms, mountains, and cities.

The enemy fears city and street wars most, a war in which the enemy expects grave human losses.

Martyrdom operations

We stress the importance of the martyrdom operations against the enemy - operations that inflicted harm on the United States and Israel that have been unprecedented in their history, thanks to Almighty God.

We also point out that whoever supported the United States, including the hypocrites of Iraq or the rulers of Arab countries, those who approved their actions and followed them in this crusade war by fighting with them or providing bases and administrative support, or any form of support, even by words, to kill the Muslims in Iraq, should know that they are apostates and outside the community of Muslims.

It is permissible to spill their blood and take their property.

God says: "O ye who believe! Take not the Jews and the Christians for your friends and protectors: they are but friends and protectors to each other."

And he amongst you that turns to them [for friendship] is of them.

Verily, Allah guideth not a people unjust.

Mobilizing the 'Islamic nation'

We also stress to honest Muslims that they should move, incite, and mobilize the [Islamic] nation, amid such grave events and hot atmosphere so as to liberate themselves from those unjust and renegade ruling regimes, which are enslaved by the United States.

They should also do so to establish the rule of God on earth.

The most qualified regions for liberation are Jordan, Morocco, Nigeria, Pakistan, the land of the two holy mosques [Saudi Arabia], and Yemen.

Needless to say, this crusade war is primarily targeted against the people of Islam.

Regardless of the removal or the survival of the socialist party or Saddam, Muslims in general and the Iraqis in particular must brace themselves for jihad against this unjust campaign and acquire ammunition and weapons.

This is a prescribed duty. God says: "[And let them pray with thee] taking all precautions and bearing arms: the unbelievers wish if ye were negligent of your arms and your baggage, to assault you in a single rush."

Fighting in support of the non-Islamic banners is forbidden.

Muslims' doctrine and banner should be clear in fighting for the sake of God. He who fights to raise the word of God will fight for God's sake.

Under these circumstances, there will be no harm if the interests of Muslims converge with the interests of the socialists in the fight against the crusaders, despite our belief in the infidelity of socialists.

The jurisdiction of the socialists and those rulers has fallen a long time ago.

Socialists are infidels wherever they are, whether they are in Baghdad or Aden.

'High morale'

The fighting, which is waging and which will be waged these days, is very much like the fighting of Muslims against the Byzantine in the past.

And the convergence of interests is not detrimental. The Muslims' fighting against the Byzantine converged with the interests of the Persians.

And this was not detrimental to the companions of the prophet.

Before concluding, we reiterate the importance of high morale and caution against false rumours, defeatism, uncertainty, and discouragement.

The prophet said: "Bring good omens and do not discourage people."

He also said: "The voice of Abu-Talhah [one of the prophet's companions] in the army is better than 100 men."

During the Al-Yarmuk Battle, a man told Khalid bin-al-Walid [an Islamic commander]: "The Byzantine soldiers are too many and the Muslims are few."

So, Khalid told him: "Shame on you. Armies do not triumph with large numbers but are defeated if the spirit of defeatism prevails."

Keep this saying before your eyes: "It is not fitting for a Prophet that he should have prisoners of war until he hath thoroughly subdued the land."

"Therefore, when ye meet the unbelievers (in fight), smite at their necks."

Your wish to the crusaders should be as came in this verse of poetry: "The only language between you and us is the sword that will strike your necks."

In the end, I advise myself and you to fear God covertly and openly and to be patient in the jihad.

Victory will be achieved with patience. I also advise myself and you to say more prayers.

O ye who believe! When ye meet a force, be firm, and call Allah in remembrance much (and often); That ye may prosper.

God, who sent the book unto the prophet, who drives the clouds, and who defeated the enemy parties, defeat them and make us victorious over them.

Our Lord! Give us good in this world and good in the Hereafter and save us from the torment of the Fire! [Koranic verse].

May God's peace and blessings be upon Prophet Muhammad and his household."

Divided Nation
August 25, 2002. Letter to the People of Afghanistan.[80]

"Praise be to God, almighty lord of the heavens and earth, beloved and omnipotent. Prayers and peace upon the imam of the *mujahidin,* our leader and master Muhammad, upon all his family and followers, and upon those who follow them in righteousness until the day of judgment.

This letter is sent to you by your brother in religion and belief, Osama bin Muhammad bin Awad bin Laden.

Peace be upon you and all God's mercy and blessings.

I send this letter to the steadfast, resilient people who wage *jihad* with the sword in one hand and the holy Qur'an in the other. You lions of the holy law, you guardians of the religion, know that God Almighty has said in His book: "God has made a promise to those among you who believe and do good deeds: He will make them successors to the land, as He did those before them."

Oh people of Afghanistan, you know that *jihad* is of the utmost value in Islam, and that with it we can gain pride and eminence in this world and the next. You know that it saves our lands, protects our sanctity, spreads justices, security, and prosperity, and plants fear in the enemies' hearts. Through it kingdoms are built, and the banner of truth flies high above all others. Oh people of Afghanistan, I am convinced that you understand theses words of mine more than anyone else, since throughout the ages no invader ever settled in your lands, since you are distinguished for your strength, defiance and fortitude in the fight, and since your doors are open only to Islam. This is because Muslims never came as colonizers or out of worldly self-interest, but as missionaries brining us back to God.

Oh people of Afghanistan, God has given you the blessing of sacrificing yourselves for Him, and you have sacrificed what is dear and precious in order to make the great words "There is no god but God and Muhammad is his messenger" a reality in your land. You didn't let global unbelief – that is, Britain, Russia, and America – penetrate your land and challenge the Muslims' pride in east and west. From my position, I can say that the great spheres [of influence] being drawn around these big countries amount to not even a mosquito's wing. Indeed, they are worthless when compared to God's power and support for the faithful *mujahidin*. Whoever doubts this should learn from the Russians how the blessed *jihad* destroyed their myth. And before them, neither the Tartars nor the English could defy the holy warriors, because the peaks of this blessed land's mountains resisted every stubborn infidel.

And by the will of God Almighty, we will soon see the fall of the unbelievers' states, at whose forefront is America, the tyrant, which has destroyed all human values and transgressed all limits, and which only understands the logic and power and war.

Power to Islam and victory to the Muslims.

Abi Abdallah"

Al-Qaeda's Overarching Strategic Communication Strategy

Al-Qaeda's overarching Strategic Communication message is carefully summarized in two, relatively short documents. The first is Usama bin Laden's October 15, 2002 statement where he delineated how his followers will apply Diplomacy, Information Operations, Military Operations, and Economic - all with the grace of Allah - to defeat America. The second overarching Strategic Communication message was delivered by Ayman al-Zawahiri on May 21, 2003. Here, he delineates a detailed al-Qaeda strategic plan.

October 15, 2002. Usama bin Laden Overarching Strategic Communication Statement.[81]

"About a year has passed since the start of the U.S. crusade declared by the U.S. president in which he led an international coalition of more than 90 nations against Afghanistan.

America is now preparing a new stage in its crusade against the Islamic world, this time against the Muslim Iraqi people to complete its scheme to divide and rupture the [Muslim] nation, rob its riches and pave the way for a greater Israel after expelling the Palestinians. . . .

Oh nation of Islam . . . whether this whole nation is targeted without distinguishing between allies or foes is no longer an issue because the enemy helped us unveil this fact. The issue now is how do we face this flagrant aggression.

If we want God to grant us victory . . . we should arm ourselves with several tools, including:

- A return to God through repentance, honest work and true intentions.

- To unite under God. If it is true that conflict and differences are the main reasons for failure, matters our nation is suffering from, it is true that unity, consensus and faith are the key to victory and the gate to domination.

- To stimulate the nation's capabilities, most important of which is the Muslim who is the fuel of battle.

- Our nation is one of the richest on Earth. Its resources have for ages been exploited to serve our enemies and conspire against our brethren. And its vast military capabilities are rusting in warehouses in Islamic nations.

- It is high time that these capabilities are freed to explode and defend the targeted faith, the violated sanctity, the tarnished honor, the raped land and the robbed riches. . . .

- The priority in this war at this stage must be against the infidels, the Americans and the Jews, who will not stop infringing upon us except through jihad.

There are also merchants and capitalists who are not any less important than others in pushing this battle forward to its aim of spreading God's religion and teachings on Earth. Your money will stop a flooding that seeks our destruction. . . .

We congratulate the Muslim nation for the daring and heroic jihad operations which our brave sons conducted in Yemen against the Christian oil tanker and in Kuwait against the American occupation and aggression forces.

By striking the oil tanker in Yemen with explosives, the attackers struck at the umbilical cord of the Christians, reminding the enemy of the bloody price they have to pay for their continued aggression on our nation and robbing our riches.

The heroic Kuwait operation also proves the level of danger that threatens U.S. forces in Islamic countries, and the political office will issue two separate statements on the two operations and their indications. . . .

The timing of the attack against a military target of such importance as Marine forces in Kuwait and the bombing of an economic target the size of the oil tanker in Yemen, and issuing oral and written statements from Taliban and Qaeda leaders who America thought it had killed. . . .

The fact that all this coincided with the one-year anniversary of the start of the Christian crusade is not a coincidence but a clear and strong message to all our enemies and friends alike that the Mujaheddin, thanks be to God, have not been weakened or exhausted and that God repaid those who sinned with their mischief.

We are continuing our path . . . and we renew our promise to God, and to the nation, and our promise to the Americans and Jews that they will not be at peace and should not dream of security until they let our nations be and stop their aggression and support for our enemies. The unjust know what awaits them."

May 21, 2003. Ayman al-Zawahiri's delineation of an al-Qaeda strategic plan.[82]

"After dividing Iraq, Saudi Arabia, Iran, Syria, and Pakistan will come next.

They would leave around Israel only dismembered semi states that are subservient to the United States and Israel.

O Muslims, these are the facts that have been made clear to you.

All the worn out and shabby masks have fallen. Here are the rulers of the Muslims with their airports, bases, and facilities.

They allow their ships to pass in their water, provide them with fuel, food, and supplies and allow their planes to cross their airspace and to even take off from their airports.

They welcome their armies to attack Iraq from their territories. The armies also advance from Kuwait.

We have Qatar where the command of the campaign has taken up its headquarters.

We also have Bahrain, which hosts the command of the Fifth Fleet.

We have Egypt where war vessels pass through its canal. And we have Yemen that supplies the crusader vessels from its ports.

And we have Jordan where the crusader forces are stationed and where Patriot missile batteries have been deployed to protect Israel.

After all this, they shout with all hypocrisy and deception that they oppose the war on Iraq.

Protests will not do you any good, neither will demonstrations or conferences.

Nothing will do you good, but toting arms and taking revenge against your enemies, the Americans and the Jews.

Demonstrations will not... protect your jeopardised holy places or expel an occupying enemy, nor will they deter an arrogant aggressor.

'Tribulation' of 9/11

The crusaders and the Jews do not understand but the language of killing and blood.

They do not become convinced unless they see coffins returning to them, their interests being destroyed, their towers being torched, and their economy collapsing.

O Muslims, take matters firmly against the embassies of America, England, Australia, and Norway and their interests, companies, and employees.

Burn the ground under their feet, as they should not enjoy your protection, safety, or security. Expel those criminals out of your countries.

Do not allow the Americans, the British, the Australians, the Norwegians, and the other crusaders who killed your brothers in Iraq to live in your countries, enjoy their resources, and wreak havoc in them.

Learn from your 19 brothers who attacked America in its planes in New York and Washington and caused it a tribulation that it never witnessed before and is still suffering from its injuries until today.

O Iraqi people, we defeated those crusaders several times before and expelled them out of our countries and holy shrines.

You should know that you are not alone in this battle. Your mujahid brothers are tracking your enemies and lying in wait for them.

The mujahideen in Palestine, Afghanistan, and Chechnya and even in the heart of America and the West are causing death to those crusaders.

The coming days will bring to you the news that will heal your breasts, God willing."

Al-Qaeda's Specific Messages for Specific Audiences

The final three messages in this book were written by al-Qaeda leadership to deliver very specific messages to very specific audiences. The first appears to be a well-scripted interview, delivered by Usama bin Laden on November 9, 2001. This interview shows Usama bin Laden warning the United States that al-Qaeda has nuclear and chemical weapon capability and will use these as retaliatory weapons. The second is a letter of disappointment from Usama bin Laden to the President of Pakistan – who has agreed to help President Bush in his fight against terrorism. The third shows Usama bin Laden arguing his point that the United States and the United Nations are dividing the world by attacking Muslims.

November 9, 2001. "Osama claims he has nukes. If US uses N-arms it will get same response" Interview by Hamid Mir with Osama bin Laden.[83]

"Hamid Mir: After American bombing on Afghanistan on Oct 7, you told the Al-Jazeera TV that the Sept 11 attacks had been carried out by some Muslims. How did you know they were Muslims ?

Osama bin Laden: The Americans themselves released a list of the suspects of the Sept 11 attacks, saying that the persons named were involved in the attacks. They were all Muslims, of whom 15 belonged to Saudi Arabia, two were from the UAE and one from Egypt. According to the information I have, they were all passengers.Fateha was held for them in their homes. But America said they were hijackers.

HM: In your statement of Oct 7, you expressed satisfaction over the Sept 11 attacks, although a large number of innocent people perished in them, hundreds among them were Muslims. Can you justify the killing of innocent men in the light of Islamic teachings ?

OBL: This is a major point in jurisprudence. In my view, if an enemy occupies a Muslim territory and uses common people as human shield, then it is permitted to attack that enemy. For instance, if bandits barge into a home and hold a child hostage, then the child's father can attack the bandits and in that attack even the child may get hurt.

America and its allies are massacring us in Palestine, Chechenya, Kashmir and Iraq. The Muslims have the right to attack America in reprisal. The Islamic Shariat says Muslims should not live in the land of the infidel for long. The Sept 11 attacks were not targeted at women and children. The real targets were America's icons of military and economic power.

The Holy Prophet (peace be upon him) was against killing women and children. When he saw a dead woman during a war, he asked why was she killed ? If a child is above 13 and wields a weapon against Muslims, then it is permitted to kill him.

The American people should remember that they pay taxes to their government, they elect their president, their government manufactures arms and gives them to Israel and Israel uses them to massacre Palestinians. The American Congress endorses all government measures and this proves that the entire America is responsible for the atrocities perpetrated against Muslims. The entire America, because they elect the Congress.

I ask the American people to force their government to give up anti-Muslim policies. The American people had risen against their government's war in Vietnam. They must do the same today. The American people should stop the massacre of Muslims by their government.

HM: Can it be said that you are against the American government, not the American people?

OSB: Yes! We are carrying on the mission of our Prophet, Muhammad (peace be upon him). The mission is to spread the word of God, not to indulge massacring people. We ourselves are the target of killings, destruction and atrocities. We are only defending ourselves. This is defensive Jihad. We want to defend our people and our land. That is why I say that if we don't get security, the Americans, too would not get security.

This is a simple formula that even an American child can understand. This is the formula of live and let live.

HM: The head of Egypt's Jamia Al-Azhar has issued a fatwa (edict) against you, saying that the views and beliefs of Osama bin Laden have nothing to do with Islam. What do you have to say about that?

OSB: The fatwa of any official Aalim has no value for me. History is full of such Ulema who justify Riba, who justify the occupation of Palestine by the Jews, who justify the presence of American troops around Harmain Sharifain. These people support the infidels for their personal gain. The true Ulema support the Jihad against America. Tell me if Indian forces invaded Pakistan what would you do? The Israeli forces occupy our land and the American troops are on our territory. We have no other option but to launch Jihad.

HM: Some Western media claim that you are trying to acquire chemical and nuclear weapons. How much truth is there in such reports?

OSB: I heard the speech of American President Bush yesterday (Oct 7). He was scaring the European countries that Osama wanted to attack with weapons of mass destruction. I wish to declare that if America used chemical or nuclear weapons against us, then we may retort with chemical and nuclear weapons. We have the weapons as deterrent.

HM: Where did you get these weapons from?

OSB: Go to the next question.

HM: Demonstrations are being held in many European countries against American attacks on Afghanistan. Thousands of the protesters were non-Muslims. What is your opinion about those non-Muslim protesters ?

OSB: There are many innocent and good-hearted people in the West. American media instigates them against Muslims. However, some good-hearted people are protesting against American attacks because human nature abhors injustice.

The Muslims were massacred under the UN patronage in Bosnia. I am ware that some officers of the State Department had resigned in protest. Many years ago the US ambassador in Egypt had resigned in protest against the policies of President Jimmy Carter. Nice and civilized are everywhere. The Jewish lobby has taken America and the West hostage.

HM: Some people say that war is no solution to any issue. Do you think that some political formula could be found to stop the present war?

OSB: You should put this question to those who have started this war. We are only defending ourselves.

HM: If America got out of Saudi Arabia and the Al-Aqsa mosque was liberated, would you then present yourself for trial in some Muslim country?

OSB: Only Afghanistan is an Islamic country. Pakistan follows the English law. I don't consider Saudi Arabia an Islamic country. If the Americans have charges against me, we too have a charge sheet against them.

HM: Pakistan government decided to cooperate with America after Sept 11, which you don't consider right. What do you think Pakistan should have done but to cooperate with America?

OSB: The government of Pakistan should have the wishes of the people in view. It should not have surrendered to the unjustified demands of America. America does not have solid proof against us. It just has some surmises. It is unjust to start bombing on the basis of those surmises.

HM: Had America decided to attack Pakistan with the help of India and Israel, what would have we done?

OSB: What has America achieved by attacking Afghanistan? We will not leave the Pakistani people and the Pakistani territory at anybody's mercy.

We will defend Pakistan. But we have been disappointed by Gen Pervez Musharraf. He says that the majority is with him. I say the majority is against him.

Bush has used the word crusade. This is a crusade declared by Bush. It is no wisdom to barter off blood of Afghan brethren to improve Pakistan's economy. He will be punished by the Pakistani people and Allah.

Right now a great war of Islamic history is being fought in Afghanistan. All the big powers are united against Muslims. It is ' sawab ' to participate in this war.

HM: A French newspaper has claimed that you had kidney problem and had secretly gone to Dubai for treatment last year. Is that correct?

OSB: My kidneys are all right. I did not go to Dubai last year. One British newspaper has published an imaginary interview with Islamabad dateline with one of my sons who lives in Saudi Arabia. All this is false.

HM: Is it correct that a daughter of Mulla Omar is your wife or your daughter is Mulla Omar's wife?

OSB: (Laughs). All my wives are Arabs (and all my daughters are married to Arab Mujahideen). I have spiritual relationship with Mulla Omar. He is a great and brave Muslim of this age. He does not fear anyone but Allah. He is not under any personal relationship or obligation to me. He is only discharging his religious duty. I, too, have not chosen this life out of any personal consideration."

November 1, 2001. Usama bin Laden letter stating disappointment of Pakistan's shifted support to the United States and the United Kingdom.[84]

"In the name of God, the most gracious, the most merciful.

My Muslim brethren in the chaste land of Pakistan, civilians and military. God's peace and blessings be upon you.

The crusade against Islam has intensified and the killing of the followers of Muhammad, may God's peace and blessings be upon him, has spread widely in Afghanistan.

The world has been divided into two camps: One under the banner of the cross, as [US President George W] Bush, the head of infidelity, said, and another under the banner of Islam.

The Pakistani Government has fallen under the banner of the cross. The Almighty God says: To the hypocrites give the glad tidings that there is for them but a grievous penalty; yea, to those who take for friends unbelievers rather than believers: Is it honour they seek among them? Nay, all honour is with God.

O supporters of Islam: This is your day to support Islam.

"Whoever believes in God and Doomsday must not rest at ease until he upholds right and its supporters and until God defeats falsehood and its backers.

Your stand against falsehood will strengthen us. But if they seek your aid in religion, it is your duty to help them. Prophet Muhammad, may God's peace and blessings be upon him, says: "A Muslim is a brother to fellow Muslims. He neither does them injustice, nor lets them down, nor surrenders them."

Let God be my witness that I have conveyed the message.

Let God be my witness that I have conveyed the message.

Let God be my witness that I have conveyed the message.

May God's peace, mercy, and blessings be upon you."

15 Shaban 1422 Hegira [1 November 2001]

Osama Bin Muhammad Bin Laden"

November 3, 2001. Usama bin Laden complains about the United States and the United Nations and warns that US/UN attacks divide the world.[85]

"We praise God, seek His help, and ask for His forgiveness.

We seek refuge in God from the evils of our souls and our bad deeds.

A person who is guided by God will never be misguided by anyone and a person who is misguided by God can never be guided by anyone.

I bear witness that there is no God but Allah alone, Who has no partner.

Attacks divide world

Amid the huge developments and in the wake of the great strikes that hit the United States in its most important locations in New York and Washington, a huge media clamour has been raised.

This clamour is unprecedented. It conveyed the opinions of people on these events.

People were divided into two parts. The first part supported these strikes against US tyranny, while the second denounced them.

Afterward, when the United States launched the unjust campaign against the Islamic Emirate in Afghanistan, people also split into two parties.

The first supported these campaigns, while the second denounced and rejected them.

These tremendous incidents, which have split people into two parties, are of great interest to the Muslims, since many of the rulings pertain to them.

The polls showed that the vast majority of the sons of the Islamic world were happy about these strikes.

Bin Laden on 11 September attacks

These rulings are closely related to Islam and the acts that corrupt a person's Islam.

Therefore, the Muslims must understand the nature and truth of this conflict so that it will be easy for them to determine where they stand.

While talking about the truth of the conflict, opinion polls in the world have shown that a little more than 80 per cent of Westerners, of Christians in the United States and elsewhere, have been saddened by the strikes that hit the United States.

The polls showed that the vast majority of the sons of the Islamic world were happy about these strikes because they believe that the strikes were in reaction to the huge criminality practiced by Israel and the United States in Palestine and other Muslim countries.

After the strikes on Afghanistan began, these groups changed positions.

Those who were happy about striking the United States felt sad when Afghanistan was hit, and those who felt sad when the United States was hit were happy when Afghanistan was hit. These groups comprise millions of people.

"Barbaric" West

The entire West, with the exception of a few countries, supports this unfair, barbaric campaign, although there is no evidence of the involvement of the people of Afghanistan in what happened in America.

The people of Afghanistan had nothing to do with this matter. The campaign, however, continues to unjustly annihilate the villagers and civilians, children, women, and innocent people.

The entire West, with the exception of a few countries, supports this unfair, barbaric campaign.

Bin Laden on the West

The positions of the two sides are very clear. Mass demonstrations have spread from the farthest point in the eastern part of the Islamic world to the farthest point in the western part of the Islamic world, and from Indonesia, Philippines, Bangladesh, India, Pakistan to the Arab world and Nigeria and Mauritania.

War "fundamentally religious"

This clearly indicates the nature of this war. This war is fundamentally religious. The people of the East are Muslims. They sympathized with Muslims against the people of the West, who are the crusaders.

Those who try to cover this crystal clear fact, which the entire world has admitted, are deceiving the Islamic nation.

They are trying to deflect the attention of the Islamic nation from the truth of this conflict.

This fact is proven in the book of God Almighty and in the teachings of our messenger, may God's peace and blessings be upon him.

Under no circumstances should we forget this enmity between us and the infidels. For, the enmity is based on creed.

Muslims must stand together

We must be loyal to the believers and those who believe that there is no God but Allah.

We should also renounce the atheists and infidels. It suffices me to seek God's help against them.

God says: "Never will the Jews or the Christians be satisfied with thee unless thou follow their form of religion."

It is a question of faith, not a war against terrorism, as Bush and Blair try to depict it.

Many thieves belonging to this nation were captured in the past. But, nobody moved.

It is a question of faith, not a war against terrorism, as Bush and Blair try to depict it.

Bin Laden on the war

The masses which moved in the East and West have not done so for the sake of Osama.

Rather, they moved for the sake of their religion. This is because they know that they are right and that they resist the most ferocious, serious, and violent Crusade campaign against Islam ever since the message was revealed to Muhammad, may God's peace and blessings be upon.

After this has become clear, the Muslim must know and learn where he is standing vis-a-vis this war.

"Crusader war"

After the US politicians spoke and after the US newspapers and television channels became full of clear crusading hatred in this campaign that aims at mobilizing the West against Islam and Muslims, Bush left no room for doubts or the opinions of journalists, but he openly and clearly said that this war is a crusader war. He said this before the whole world to emphasize this fact.

Anyone who lines up behind Bush in this campaign has committed one of the 10 actions that sully one's Islam.

Bin Laden names names

What can those who allege that this is a war against terrorism say? What terrorism are they speaking about at a time when the Islamic nation has been slaughtered for tens of years without hearing their voices and without seeing any action by them?

But when the victim starts to take revenge for those innocent children in Palestine, Iraq, southern Sudan, Somalia, Kashmir and the Philippines, the rulers' ulema (Islamic leaders) and the hypocrites come to defend the clear blasphemy. It suffices me to seek God's help against them.

The common people have understood the issue, but there are those who continue to flatter those who colluded with the unbelievers to anesthetized the Islamic nation to prevent it from carrying out the duty of jihad so that the word of God will be above all words.

The unequivocal truth is that Bush has carried the cross and raised its banner high and stood at the front of the queue.

Anyone who lines up behind Bush in this campaign has committed one of the 10 actions that sully one's Islam.

Muslim scholars are unanimous that allegiance to the infidels and support for them against the believers is one of the major acts that sully Islam.

Latest stage in "Crusade"

There is no power but in God. Let us investigate whether this war against Afghanistan that broke out a few days ago is a single and unique one or if it is a link to a long series of crusader wars against the Islamic world.

Following World War I, which ended more than 83 years ago, the whole Islamic world fell under the crusader banner - under the British, French, and Italian governments.

They divided the whole world, and Palestine was occupied by the British.

Since then, and for more than 83 years, our brothers, sons, and sisters in Palestine have been badly tortured.

Hundreds of thousands of them have been killed, and hundreds of thousands of them have been imprisoned or maimed.

"Crusade" against Chechens

Let us examine the recent developments. Take for example the Chechens.

They are a Muslim people who have been attacked by the Russian bear which embraces the Christian Orthodox faith.

Russians have annihilated the Chechen people in their entirety and forced them to flee to the mountains where they were assaulted by snow and poverty and diseases.

Nonetheless, nobody moved to support them. There is no strength but in God.

"Crusade" against Bosnia

This was followed by a war of genocide in Bosnia in sight and hearing of the entire world in the heart of Europe.

For several years our brothers have been killed, our women have been raped, and our children have been massacred in the safe havens of the United Nations and with its knowledge and cooperation.

Those who refer our tragedies today to the United Nations so that they can be resolved are hypocrites who deceive God, His Prophet and the believers.

UN "collusion"

Are not our tragedies but caused by the United Nations? Who issued the Partition Resolution on Palestine in 1947 and surrendered the land of Muslims to the Jews? It was the United Nations in its resolution in 1947.

Those who claim that they are the leaders of the Arabs and continue to appeal to the United Nations have disavowed what was revealed to Prophet Muhammad, God's peace and blessings be upon him.

Those who refer things to the international legitimacy have disavowed the legitimacy of the Holy Book and the tradition of Prophet Muhammad, God's peace and blessings be upon him.

This is the United Nations from which we have suffered greatly. Under no circumstances should any Muslim or sane person resort to the United Nations. The United Nations is nothing but a tool of crime.

We are being massacred everyday, while the United Nations continues to sit idly by.

Kashmir and Chechens

Our brothers in Kashmir have been subjected to the worst forms of torture for over 50 years. They have been massacred, killed, and raped. Their blood has been shed and their houses have been trespassed upon.

Still, the United Nations continues to sit idly by.

Today, and without any evidence, the United Nations passes resolutions supporting unjust and tyrannical America, which oppresses these helpless people who have emerged from a merciless war at the hands of the Soviet Union.

Let us look at the second war in Chechnya, which is still underway. The entire Chechen people are being embattled once again by this Russian bear.

The humanitarian agencies, even the US ones, demanded that President Clinton should stop supporting Russia.

However, Clinton said that stopping support for Russia did not serve US interests.

A year ago, Putin demanded that the cross and the Jews should stand by him. He told them: You must support us and thank us because we are waging a war against Muslim fundamentalism.

The enemies are speaking very clearly. While this is taking place, the leaders of the region hide and are ashamed to support their brothers.

East Timor and Somalia

Let us examine the stand of the West and the United Nations in the developments in Indonesia when they moved to divide the largest country in the Islamic world in terms of population.

We should view events not as separate links, but as links in a long series of conspiracies, a war of annihilation.

Bin Laden on "Crusade"

This criminal, Kofi Annan, was speaking publicly and putting pressure on the Indonesian government, telling it: You have 24 hours to divide and separate East Timor from Indonesia.

Otherwise, we will be forced to send in military forces to separate it by force.

The crusader Australian forces were on Indonesian shores, and in fact they landed to separate East Timor, which is part of the Islamic world.

Therefore, we should view events not as separate links, but as links in a long series of conspiracies, a war of annihilation in the true sense of the word.

In Somalia, on the excuse of restoring hope, 13,000 of our brothers were killed. In southern Sudan, hundreds of thousands were killed.

Palestinians and Iraqis

But when we move to Palestine and Iraq, there can be no bounds to what can be said.

Over one million children were killed in Iraq. The killing is continuing.

As for what is taking place in Palestine these days, I can only say we have no one but God to complain to.

What is taking place cannot be tolerated by any nation. I do not say from the nations of the human race, but from other creatures, from the animals. They would not tolerate what is taking place.

A confidant of mine told me that he saw a butcher slaughtering a camel in front of another camel.

The other camel got agitated while seeing the blood coming out of the other camel. Thus, it burst out with rage and bit the hand of the man and broke it.

How can the weak mothers in Palestine endure the killing of their children in front of their eyes by the unjust Jewish executioners with US support and with US aircraft and tanks?

Israel and US "are one"

Those who distinguish between America and Israel are the real enemies of the nation. They are traitors who betrayed God and His prophet, and who betrayed their nation and the trust placed in them. They anesthetize the nation.

These battles cannot be viewed in any case whatsoever as isolated battles, but rather, as part of a chain of the long, fierce, and ugly crusader war.

Every Muslim must stand under the banner of There is no God but Allah and Muhammad is God's Prophet.

I remind you of what our Prophet, may God's peace and blessings upon him, told Ibn Abbas, may God be pleased with him.

He told him: Boy, I am going to teach you a few words. Obey God, He will protect you. Obey Him, you will find Him on your side. If you ask for something, ask God. If you seek help, seek the help of God.

You should know that if all people come together to help you, they will only help you with something that God has already preordained for you.

And if they assemble to harm you, they will only harm you with something that God has already preordained for you. God wrote man's fate and it will never change.

I Tell the Muslims who did their utmost during these weeks: You must continue along the same march.

Your support for us will make us stronger and will further support your brothers in Afghanistan.

Exert more efforts in combating this unprecedented war crime.

Fear God, O Muslims and rise to support your religion. Islam is calling on you: O Muslims, O Muslims, O Muslims.

God bear witness that I have conveyed the message. God bear witness that I have conveyed the message. God bear witness that I have conveyed the message.

God's peace and blessings be upon you."

Chapter 4
Strategic Communication Efforts
by the West

The Global War on Terror is being communicated to the public through a combined White House, Department of State and Department of Defense Strategic Communication Plan. Similarly, many Friends and Allies of the West are implementing their own (or multinational, coordinated) Strategic Communication plans. Whether these plans are being successfully executed is debatable. But the fact that an ongoing effort to communicate themes and messages to our friends, allies and enemies exists is indisputable. Strategic Communication is a potentially valuable tool to help shape the world into a better place to live. While the concept of Strategic Communication is still inchoate, it has evolved considerably in the past few years and will undoubtedly continue to expand.

Usama bin Laden and Ayman al-Zawahiri Were Not the First to Try Applying Their Interpretation of Morals, Ethics and Religion into a Strategic Communication Theme… Not By A Long Shot

The United States, as a nation, believes in the concept of "Just Wars." We only need listen to President Bush using terms such as "punish evildoers" and "secure the peace" to re-affirm where his thoughts originate. Similarly, Muslim extremists believe they are engaged in a version of "Just War." The different interpretations of the same concept by these two diametrically opposed organizations drives the United States towards the necessity to carefully assess the strategy, tactics and procedures necessary to defeat the enemy. The United States, using a different set of guidelines than our enemy to define "Just War" will need to carefully balance Civil Rights and expected freedoms with national security.

Successful Strategic Communication Plans Must Include an Appreciation of the Past (and Consider How "Just War Theory" Applies)

The Turkish Islamic Scholar, Ahmet Hamdi Yazir, supports the theory that "Jihad" can only be waged for freedom of religion and not for general war.[86] Furthermore, he references 2:256 of the Qur'an, which states "Let there be no compulsion in religion; Truth stands out clear from error; whoever rejects evil and believes in God hath grasped the most trustworthy hand-hold that never breaks. And God heareth and knoweth all things."[87] Another Islamic expert and historian, Abdullah Yusuf Ali, in his 1938 self-translated and published version of the Qur'an states "Compulsion is incompatible with religion. Because religion depends upon faith and will, which would be meaningless if induced with force."[88] Conversely, Osama bin-Laden, in his 1998 Fatwa directs all Americans and Jews be killed without discrimination between combatants and non-combatants, women, children or men.[89]

Just War Theory

Telford Taylor. No person in the past seventy-five years, military or civilian, has studied (and for practical reasons applied) the concept of "Just War" and "Unjust War" more thoroughly than Brigadier General Telford Taylor. Taylor, the United States Chief Counsel at the Nuremberg Trials went to great lengths to understand the history, politics, theology and philosophy surrounding this concept.[90] The laws of war, according to Taylor, are mostly developed by military personnel who actually fight the wars.[91] Conversely, "...the principles concerning the morals or legal legitimacy of war itself have been the work of theologians, jurists, and in more recent years of diplomats."[92]

St. Augustine. St. Augustine of Hippo (AD 354-430) is the first known theologian to develop and articulate a clear doctrine of "Just and Unjust Wars." He believed it was "possible to please God while engaged in military service."[93] According to Augustine, "Just Wars are usually defined as those which avenge injuries when the nation or city against which warlike actions is to be directed has neglected to punish wrongs committed by its own citizens or to restore what has been unjustly taken by it."[94] The true aim of war, according to Augustine, is peace, "so that after the resisting nations have been conquered provision may more easily be made for enjoying in peace the mutual bond of piety and justice."[95]

St. Thomas Aquinas. 900 years later, St Thomas Aquinas (1225-1274) improved upon St. Augustine's doctrine by writing *Summa Theologiae*. *Summa Theologiae* ("In order that a war may be just") required three tenets for a Just War: First, the war must be undertaken at the direction of the prince or leader of a nation, and not by an individual. This is because individuals do not speak for the state. Secondly, there must be a just cause. Just cause, according to Aquinas, means "...those attacked must, by a fault, deserve to be attacked."[96] The third and final tenet, for a Just War centers on the concept of intent. Specifically, those who will be engaged in warfare must be motivated in order for a "good to be effected" or "evil to be avoided."[97] In the end, peace must be the object of their intention.[98]

Francisco Suarez. Francisco Suarez (1548-1617) was the first theologian to tie law, morality and doctrine together on an individual and national level by offering that war is justified (and perhaps a duty) if it: "defends life, defends property or aids a third party unjustly attacked."[99]

Frank Kellog and Aristide Briand. Some 1500 years after St. Augustine's work and 700 years after St. Thomas Aquinas' tenets, Frank Kellog of the United States and Aristide Briand of France added significantly to St. Augustine's doctrine by condemning "recourse to war for the solution of international controversies."[100] More significantly, these two men offered a fresh view towards the morality of warfare by suggesting "just and unjust wars" be replaced by "aggressive and defensive wars."[101] In August of 1928 the Kellog-Briand Pact, also known as the "Pact of Paris", reiterated and strengthened the 1927 "International Treaty of the Renunciation of War as an Instrument of National Policy." Key to the Pact, signed by 43 countries including France and the United States, was treating any war of aggression as an international crime and strictly prohibiting all acts of aggression.[102] Unfortunately, the League of Nations did not have the military or economic power to enforce such a pact, which was based on nations governing their own actions. After World War II, however, former Secretary of War Henry L. Stimson and Justice Robert L. Jackson used the aggressive and defensive war approach to prosecute Nazis and Japanese in Nuremberg and Tokyo respectively.[103]

The Catholic Church. Joseph McKenna, in his 1960 book, *Ethics and War: A Catholic View*, expanded St. Thomas Aquinas' three conditions of Just War to seven conditions. They are: (1) The war must be declared by the duly constituted authority; (2) The seriousness of injury inflicted on the enemy must be proportional to the damage suffered by the virtuous; (3) The injury to the aggressor must be real and immediate; (4) There must be a reasonable chance of winning the war; (5) The use of war must be a last resort; (6) The participants must have right intentions; and (7) The means used must be moral.[104] A 1993 document provided by the National Conference of Catholic Bishops and summarized by Reverend Hehir in an interview on National Public Radio, stated that lethal force may be used when all seven of Joseph McKenna's conditions are met, which fundamentally means war must be a last resort to defend yourself or others requiring protection.[105] The "last resort" interpretation is why Pope John Paul II, who supported actions against terrorism in Afghanistan, vehemently disagreed with President Bush and appealed as late as March 5, 2003 for the President to reconsider allowing the inspections for Weapons of Mass Destruction to run their fullest possible course before taking military action.[106]

Both the Vatican and the President of U.S. Catholic Bishops support the United States' determination in fighting the Global War on Terrorism. Joaquin Navarro-Valls, the papal spokesman for the Vatican, offered the following in October of 2001: "The use of force against terrorists by the United States and our allies can be "an action of active prevention against a threat that has already occurred in the horror of a few weeks ago and can happen again"."[107] Similarly, Bishop Joseph Fiorenza, President of the United States Conference of Catholic Bishops, wrote to President Bush to affirm the United States' ""moral right" and grave obligation to defend the common good in the face of terrorism." The Bishop continued his letter to the President reminding the National leader "to respect just-war principles," paying particular attention to "probability of success," "civilian immunity," and "proportionality."[108]

Other Religions' Views. Robert P. George, professor of Jurisprudence at Princeton University and author of *In Defense of Natural Law*, states, "The just-war theory is a common patrimony of Catholic, Protestant, and Orthodox Christians."[109] "Moreover, the teachings of Jewish tradition on war and peace are closely in line with it." It is true that modern Popes have invoked it and offered significant contributions to the theory, but it is "by no means uniquely Catholic."[110] The National Council of Synagogues and the U.S. Catholic Bishops' Committee for Ecumenical and Inter-religious Affairs stated, "...our traditions of just war...demand that even just wars be fought with concern for the lives of the innocents and for the safety and well being of noncombatants and their property."[111]

Just War Today. Just War Theory today centers on three topics: (1) The Cause of War (jus ad bellum); (2) The Conduct of War (jus in bello); and (3) The Consequences of War (jus post bellum). The major issues surrounding *jus in bello* are discriminating between combatants and non-combatants and calibrating proportionality in such a manner that a war can come to an end without high potential of revenge attacks due to atrocities or lack of proportionality during the conflict. Before the first shot is fired, there are several key factors to consider in the causality of war (jus ad bellum). The war must be authorized by a competent and authorized official (usually the leader of a nation state). Additionally, there must be just cause, appropriate intent, a reasonable expectation to win, and the use of military force must be a last resort.[112] Finally, the Consequences of War, known in scholastic circles as *Post Bellum*, are the most important considerations when determining whether to go to war (short of defending against attack). An end state and exit strategy are critical to ensuring the nation being invaded is left better (from the perspective of the local population as well as our vital national interest) than when the conquerors arrived. Failure to consider this last step of conflict could easily lead to unnecessary suffering and a quagmire situation on the battlefield.

The Muslim scholar, Bassam Tibi, offers the following morally and logically flawed statement when discussing Jihad and the West:

> The Western distinction between just and unjust wars linked to specific grounds for war is unknown in Islam. Any war against unbelievers, whatever its immediate ground, is morally justified. Only in this sense can one distinguish just and unjust wars in the Islamic tradition. When Muslims wage war...for the dissemination of Islam, it is a Just War...When non-Muslims attack Muslims, it is an unjust war. The usual Western interpretation of jihad as a "Just War" in the Western sense is, therefore, a misreading of the Islamic concept.[113]

It is clear why those less-educated are confused about moral righteousness and simple logic, when the supposed scholars make statements such as this. This thought process, and the poor track record of Muslims throughout history led Samuel P. Huntington, Harvard Professor and author of *Clash of the Civilizations* to offer the following observation:

> Wherever one looks along the perimeter of Islam, Muslims have problems living peaceably with their neighbors. The question naturally rises as to whether

this pattern of late-twentieth-century conflict between Muslim and non-Muslim groups is equally true of relations between groups from other civilizations. In fact, it is not. Muslims make up for one-fifth of the world's population but in the 1990s they have been far more involved in intergroup violence than the people of any other civilization. The evidence is overwhelming.[114]

Morality, Religion and Ethics aside, terrorists groups, like the one that attacked America on September 11, 2001, are in direct violation of international law. Without delving into great detail, the following International Laws concerning the Bombing of Civilians were violated on 9-11 alone: Article XXII, XXIII, XXV, XXVI and XXVII of the Laws and Customs of War on Land (Hague, II) July 29, 1899 (updated on October 18, 1907 in Hague, IV and again in 1923). Additionally, Articles VI, VII, and VIII of the August 8, 1945 Nuremberg Principles were violated. The Geneva Convention of 1949, Articles XII, XIII and XVI were violated. And finally, with the recent Fatwa implying that any means of attack is acceptable, the July 8, 1996 Hague Convention bans the use or threat of use of nuclear weapons (especially against civilian targets).[115]

Defeating Terrorism requires we first understand those who perpetuate hatred against the "Crusaders". Kenneth Timmerman, in his book, *Preacher's of Hate*, correctly states "We are not faced with a social problem, which liberal policies and public money can solve; we are facing dedicated murderers. If we are to craft serious and effective policies to combat them, we must begin by recognizing the uncompromising depths of their hatred."[116]

A 1990 RAND study, entitled U.S. Countermeasures Against International Terrorism, correctly suggests that while terrorism will never be "completely eliminated", the threat may be reduced significantly by employing the correct countermeasures in the right sequence.[117] Michael Ledeen, in his book entitled *The War Against The Terror Masters* breaks the difficult task of defending America (he wrongly calls it "winning the war") into three conceivable actions: (1) "Secure the Homeland; (2) kill or incarcerate the terrorists; and (3) bring down the terror masters-those supplying or assisting the terrorists."[118] While this book, and more than 100 other books and articles we have read searching for the right combination to counter terrorism, offers many good ideas, only one publication (*Fighting Terrorism* by Benjamin Netanyahu) clearly articulates an executable plan to significantly deter the threat of international terrorism while maintaining a civil society.[119] Interestingly, this book was first published in 1995 and updated in the aftermath of the September 11th attacks.

Chapter 5
Conclusion

This book can be consolidated into several key points:

1) Strategic communication must be understood as an art and a science before it can be successfully applied. Strategic communication far exceeds mere words and media efforts. It is a combination of words and deeds carefully crafted and executed in a manner which delivers themes and messages and ultimately supports the goals of an organization. Strategic communication is often understood to be a combination of information operations, media/public affairs efforts and the incorporation of public diplomacy. These three enablers can only achieve the organization's goals if they are applied together as one strategic roadmap with a singular vision (goal) in mind.

2) Successful application of strategic communication requires intelligent, normally well-educated, and always highly-motivated, message-focused communicators. Usama bin Laden and Ayman

al-Zawahiri are the most recent, in a series of communicators, to attempt to influence the world through word and deed. In the past several decades alone, Karl Marx and Adolf Hitler both made similar efforts with varying degrees of success. Karl Marx's *Communist Manifesto* and Adolf Hitler's *Mein Kampf*, similar to Usama bin Laden's *Fatwas* of 1996 and 1998, and Ayman al-Zawahiri's *Knights under the Prophet's Banner* and *The Bitter Harvest*, contain common threads of likeminded individuals with global ambitions. Karl Marx was raised in an aristocratic family, where he received a world-class education at the University of Berlin. He earned a PhD in philosophy and studied law. Adolf Hilter, while not formally educated, was well-read and a serious student of modern politics. Usama bin Laden attended King Abdul al-Aziz University where he studied economics. Usama bin Laden, like Karl Marx, was raised in a wealthy and aristocratic household. Dr. Ayman al-Zawahiri is similarly well-educated and holds a Medical Degree and has been certified as a surgeon. All of these individuals used their education (whether formal or not) to better understand and shape their environment through words and deeds.

3) History demonstrates that a successful strategic communicator, who can win the hearts and minds of the population, can create an army with nearly unlimited potential. It is inconceivable that Hitler could lead Germany into World War II, but his ability to communicate a message did just that.

4) The "winner" of the strategic communication war has the potential to seriously challenge an adversary (whether that adversary is

technologically superior or not); even if the adversary controls substantially more resources than the challenger.

5) Our world is "shaped" through diplomacy, information dissemination, military application, economic and financial efforts, understanding the dynamics of the world through intelligence and the careful implementation of international agreements and treaties through the judicious application of law enforcement. These enablers can only be successfully applied with a robust and well-conceived strategic communication plan.

Understanding the Impact of Strategic Communication

1) Strategic communication must be understood as an art and a science before it can be successfully applied.

2) Successful application of strategic communication requires intelligent, normally well-educated, and always highly-motivated, message-focused communicators.

3) History demonstrates that a successful strategic communicator, who can win the hearts and minds of the population, can create an army with nearly unlimited potential.

4) The "winner" of the strategic communication war has the potential to seriously challenge an adversary (whether that adversary is technologically superior or not); even if the adversary controls substantially more resources than the challenger.

5) Our world is "shaped" through diplomacy, information dissemination, military application, economic and financial efforts, understanding the dynamics of the world through intelligence and the careful implementation of international agreements and treaties through the judicious application of law enforcement. These enablers can only be successfully applied with a robust and well-conceived strategic communication plan.

Notes

Note: Usama bin Laden is also referred to as "UBL" throughout the following notes.

[1] This 1998 interview with UBL was posted to the Free Republic website on October 7, 2001.; http://www.freerepublic.com/focus/f-news/452192/posts.

[2] Al-Arabiya television. London. August 3, 2003. http://www.tribuneinida.com/2003/20030804/world.htm#2.

[3] This 1998 interview with UBL was posted to the Free Republic website on October 7, 2001.; http://www.freerepublic.com/focus/f-news/452192/posts.

[4] Al-Arabiya television. London. August 3, 2003. http://www.tribuneinida.com/2003/20030804/world.htm#2.

[5] The authors wish to thank Mr. Hank Cormier and Ms. Tracy Roou for their insight, collegial support, and permission to restate some of the earlier shared research on this issue. Earlier efforts by Dr. Parker, Ms. Roou and Mr. Cormier resulted in a paper focused on comparing Hitler, Marx and Bin-Laden. These ideas are expanded upon in this document.

[6] This treaty sought punitive actions towards Germany to ensure the state was incapable of future aggression.

[7] The authors believe that many well-intentioned, and well-educated, moderate Muslims do not support this "Jihadist approach to peace".

[8] As mentioned in endnote 5 above, this paragraph is a result of an earlier collaborative effort by Dr. Parker, Ms. Roou and Mr. Cormier. Ms. Roou and Mr. Cormier kindly approved reiteration and reproduction of this effort in the book you are reading.

[9] Marx, Lenin and Stalin were particularly good writers. However, Hitler's *Mein Kampf* is poorly written and often rambles on. Hitler's follow-on book (*Book 2*)

provides a clearer picture of "Hitler, the Conqueror". Book 2 was completed in 1928, but was not published until after the Fuhrer's death.

[10] UBL's effectiveness as a fighter alongside the mujahadeen is debated. The fact that he was an active participant in the battles is not. According to our assessment of ABC reporter, John Miller's May 1998 interview with Osama bin Laden, the future leader of al-Qaeda appeared to be well-respected as a freedom fighter. Of course bin Laden himself, speaks of his many courageous acts. We, the authors, were unable to validate these acts beyond the al-Qaeda leader's personal statements. The following quote originated at http://www.pbs.org/wgbh/pages/frontline/shows/binladen/who/miller.html

"On December 25, 1979, the Soviet Union invaded Afghanistan. Bin Laden, then twenty-two, left for the fighting immediately. When he arrived, he wasted no time. Spending his money, he financed the recruitment, transportation, and arming of thousands of Palestinians, Tunisians, Somalians, Egyptians, Saudis, and Pakistanis to fight the Russians. Bin Laden brought in his own bulldozers and dump trucks. Grizzled mujahideen fighters still tell of the young man who rode the bulldozers himself, digging trenches on the front lines. The men who follow bin Laden have all heard the stories, and they pass them on to the younger men. By his own account, he was in the thick of the action. He says he got the rifle he carries now in hand-to-hand combat. "We went through vicious battles with the Russians," bin Laden told me. "The Russians are known for their brutality. They used poison gases against us. I was subjected to this. We lost many fighters. But we were able to deter many commando attacks, unlike anything before.""

[11] Edward M. Collins. *Myth, Manifesto, Meltdown*. pg. 7-9.

[12] Robert Conquest. *Where Marx Went Wrong*. pg. 21-25.

[13] http://www.bbc.co.uk/history/historic_figures/marx_karl.shtml.

[14] There is a strong parallel between the messages of Military Strategists, Clausewitz, and those of Adolf Hitler.

[15] Mein Kampf is loosely translated as, "My struggle" or "My battle" and was not Hilter's first choice. Hitler was convinced by his publisher not to use his original title, "*Four and a half years of struggle against lies, stupidity, and cowardice*". (This issue is discussed in greater detail by Philip Greenspun on his website http://philip.greenspun.com)

[16] Hitler's close friend Ernst Hanfstaengl stated in his memoirs that Hitler could, "quote Clausewitz by the yard." Hitler's opening lines in Chapter XV, entitled "The Right of Emergency Defense," quotes Clausewitz directly.

> "That the stain of a cowardly submission can never be effaced; that this drop of poison in the blood of a people is passed on to posterity and will paralyze and undermine the strength of later generations; that, on the other hand, even the loss of this freedom after a bloody and horrible struggle assures the rebirth of a people and is the seed of life from which some day a new tree will strike fast roots."

The above paragraph clearly explicates Hitler's feelings regarding post-World War I Germany. Clearly, Hitler intended to demonstrate that while Germans lost WWI, they were not cowards and their future was bright.

In addition to Clausewitz, Hitler references Gobineau's 1854 Essay on the Inequality of the Human Races as he delineates his plan for a "master race". Similarly, he borrows many ideas from Houston Chamberlain's 1898 book entitled Foundations of the Nineteenth Century. While the self-educated Hitler was well read, it is as likely that Hess, with his formal education, was the true author of Mein Kampf. Some historians believe Hitler never actually wrote Mein Kampf, but instead orally presented his universal beliefs to Rudolf Hess, who interpreted and wrote the document. Hess, a graduate of the University of Munich, was influenced by the Thule Society, a secret anti-Semitic political organization devoted to Nordic supremacy. Following Goring, Hess was the number three man under Hitler. A long time friendship and clear allegiance to the Fuhrer did not deter Hitler from ordering Hess to be arrested following Hess' attempt to fly to Scotland in 1941 to negotiate a peace treaty.

[17] Beer-hall PUTSCH was an ill-fated coup d-etat which began on November 8, 1923 and was quelled in less than 48 hours after Hilter failed to seize power in Munich.

[18] http://www.culteducation.com/binladen.html

[19] It is believed that Zawahiri became friends with "The Blind Sheikh" while in prison. For more details on this topic see the Global Security article at the following website http://www.globalsecurity.org/military/world/para/zawahiri.htm.

[20] The full transcript of this speech can be found at: http://www.defenselink.mil/speeches. This speech was presented by Deputy Secretary of Defense Gordon England to an Export Control Conference in October of 2006.

[21] DepSecDef. The Honorable Gordon England. Center for Strategic and International Studies, 1 February 2006 St. Regis Hotel, Washington, D.C.

[22] Ambassador Karen Hughes is the National Director of Strategic Communications. She was appointed to this position by President George W. Bush in 2005.

[23] Department of State Strategic Communications website. http://www.state.gov/r/pa/scp/

[24] Joint Publication 1-02, Department of Defense Dictionary of Military and Associated Terms, April, 2001. This publication can be found on the Joint Electronic Library online.

[25] The National Military Strategic Plan for the War on Terrorism, 1 February 2006. http://www.defenselink.mil/qdr/docs/2006-02-08-Strategic-Plan.pdf

[26] Joint Publication 3-53, Joint Doctrine for Psychological Operations, 05 September 2003. This document can be found on the Joint Electronic Library.

[27] Joint Publication 3-61, Public Affairs, 5 May 2005. This document can be found on the Joint Electronic Library.

[28] Joint Publication 3-13, Information Operations. 13 February 2006. This publication can be found in the Joint Electronic Library and delineates specific Information Operations requirements for Combatant Commanders in the Department of Defense.

[29] http://www.fbi.gov/wanted/terrorists/terbinladen.htm

[30] National Counterterrorism Center. Counterterrorism Calendar 2006. p. 4.

[31] Maryanne Weaver. "*Blowback, an unattributed biography of Bin Ladin.*"

[32] *Through our Enemies' Eyes*, Bin Laden in a 1997 interview with Hamid Mir, pg 81.

[33] According to a June 10, 1999 Interview of UBL by Jamal Isma'il (and presented by Salah Najm). UBL claims to have studied economics at Jeddah University. Jeddah University is also known as King Abdul Al-Aziz's University in Saudi Arabia.

[34] Christiane Amanpour of CNN's report entitled, "In the Footsteps of Bin Laden".

[35] Bruce Lawrence goes into detail discussing the background of MAK and the relationship between UBL and Zawahiri. pp.76-7.

[36] http://lexicorient.com/e.o/osama_b_laden.htm

[37] Miniter, Richard. *Disinformation.* p 13.

[38] Miniter, Richard. *Disinformation.* p 14.

[39] Miniter, Richard. *Disinformation.* p 14.

[40] Ibid.

[41] Did the U.S. "Create" Osama bin Laden?. January 14, 2005. http://usinfo.state.gov/media/Archive/2005/Jan/24-318760.html.

[42] http://usinfo.state.gov/media/Archive/2005/Jan/24-318760.html. This website appears to be an attempt by the Department of State to provide a strategic communication message to the United States, our friends and allies explicating that the United States has never supported UBL, his organization or his activities.

[43] National Counterterrorism Center. Counterterrorism Calendar 2006. p. 2. This page remains in quotes to credit the work of the National Counterterrorism Center.

[44] http://www.tkb.org/Group.jsp?groupID=4416

[45] http://www.fbi.gov/wanted/terrorists/teralzawahiri.htm

[46] ibid

[47] ibid

[48] According to the FBI's Most Wanted Terrorist Page, "Al-Zawahiri is a physician and the founder of the Egyptian Islamic Jihad (EIJ). This organization opposes the secular Egyptian Government and seeks its overthrow through violent means. In approximately 1998, the EIJ led by Al-Zawahiri merged with Al Qaeda." http://www.fbi.gov/wanted/terrorists/teralzawahiri.htm.

[49] Nimrod Raphlei. The Journal entitled: Terrorism and Political Violence. Dr. Raphlei is a Senior Analyst at MEMRI's Middle East Economic Studies Program. 2002 winter edition.

[50] Wright, Lawrence. *The Looming Tower: Al-Qaeda and the Road to 9/11*. Publisher: Alfred Knopf. New York, 2007. p. 259-60.

[51] Jihad Against Jews and Crusaders. 23 February 1998. http://www.fas.org/irp/world/para/docs/980223-fatwa.htm.

[52] http://www.nndb.com/people/669/000023600/.

[53] The authors were unable to confirm Ayman al-Zawahiri's wealth. However, data points imply he lived comfortably, but not with great wealth, as a surgeon in Cairo prior to his arrest in 1981. It is equally fair to assume that Ayman al-Zawahiri has access to significant funds through the al-Qaeda organization and UBL himself.

[54] Profile of Ayman al-Zawahiri: http://english.aljazeera.net/English/archive/archive?ArchiveId=2567.

[55] FBI Most Wanted Terrorist Page. http://www.fbi.gov/wanted/terrorists/terbinladen.htm. There is no mention of the September 11, 2001 attacks on this webpage.

[56] According to the book, *Through Our Enemies Eyes*, (pg. 90) UBL reported to Al-Quds Al-Arabi that he fled to Lahore, Pakistan following the Soviet Invasion.

[57] Sohail H. Hashmi, Islamic Political Ethics (Amana Publications, 2003) 217.

[58] www.IslamTomorrow.com, dictionary.

[59] Kelsay, John. *Islam and War: A Study in Comparative Ethics* (Westminister John Knoz Press, 1993) 17.

[60] Abdullah Yusuf Ali, *Holy Qur'an: Text, Translations, and Commentary* (Amana Corp., 1991) 861.

[61] Kelsay, John. *Islam and War: A Study in Comparative Ethics* (Westminister John Knoz Press, 1993) 34.

[62] Quoted in Elshtain, *Just War Against Terror*, 131.

[63] This text is a fatwa by Osama bin Laden. It was originally published in *Al Quds Al Arabi*, in August 1996.

[64] Caner, Ergun Mehmet and Emir Fethi Caner, *Unveiling Islam*, pp. 181-84.

[65] Ranstorp, Magnus, "Interpreting the Broader Context and Meaning of Bin-Laden's Fatwa." *Studies in Conflict and Terrorism*, p. 326.

[66] This statement was written by UBL and senior leadership in the Jihadist movement. It demands killing Americans - civilian and military. Published in *Al-Quds al-'Arabi* on February 23, 1998.

[67] http://www.ctc.usma.edu/harmony.asp. US Counterterrorism Center.

[68] Transcript of December 13, 2001 videotape of UBL. This document can be found in numerous locations to include: http://fl1.findlaw.com/news.findlaw.com/hdocs/docs/binladen/binladenvid121301rls.pdf.

[69] Transcript of December 13, 2001 videotape of UBL. This document can be found in numerous locations to include: http://fl1.findlaw.com/news.findlaw.com/hdocs/docs/binladen/binladenvid121301rls.pdf.

[70] As stated by UBL in 1997, in an interview with Hamid Mir. UBL is quoted as saying, "I worked on the expansion of the Al-Aqasa Mosque. During the early years of my life, I received training in the use of explosives for construction work and demolition of mountains."

[71] June 10, 1999 (date aired). Interview by Jamal Isma'il of UBL in an undisclosed location within Afghanistan. http://web.archive.org/web/20021113111503/http://www.terrorism.com/terrorism/BinLadinTranscript.shtml.

[72] Ummat, Urdu-language daily newspaper based in Karachi, Pakistan - Friday, September 28, 2001. p. 1, 7.

[73] October, 2001. Tayseer Alouni, Al-Jazeera television correspondent, interview with Osama Bin Laden. Translated by CNN. http://archives.cnn.com/2002/WORLD/asiapcf/south/02/05/binladen.transcript/index.html.

[74] October 6, 2002. Bin Laden: "Evil brings evil." http://www.newwartimes.com/laden2.html.

[75] This letter appeared on November 24, 2002 in the Observer Worldview in the United Kingdom.

[76] October 29, 2004. A message to Pre-Midterm Election America. This text was number 811 of The Middle East Media Research Institute. http://www.memri. org/bin/opener.cgi?Page=archives&ID=SP81104

[77] November 12, 2002. Letter to America's Allies. http://news.bbc.co.uk/2/hi/ middle_east/2455845.stm. In addition to the quote found in this book, BBC offers additional commentary on their website

[78] April 15, 2004. Post-Madrid Bombing: Letter to the People of Europe. http:// news.bbc.co.uk/2/hi/middle_east/3628069.stm. In addition to the quote found in this book, BBC provides additional commentary on their website pertaining to this subject.

[79] February 11, 2003. Message to the Muslim People in Iraq. http://news.bbc. co.uk/2/hi/middle_east/2751019.stm.

[80] August 25, 2002. Letter to the People of Afghanistan. Bruce Lawrence, in his book, *Messages to the World: The Statements of Osama Bin Laden*, provided a different view of UBL's August 25, 2002 message to the Afghan People.

[81] This translated excerpt by UBL was found on the WashingtonPost.com website. http://www.washingtonpost.com/ac2/wp-dyn/A25582-2002Oct14?language=pri nter

[82] May 21, 2003. http://news.bbc.co.uk/2/hi/middle_east/3047903.stm.

[83] November 9, 2001. "Osama claims he has nukes. If US uses N-arms it will get same response" Interview by Hamid Mir with UBL. http://www.dawn.com/2001/11/10/ top1.htm.

[84] November 1, 2001. UBL letter stating disappointment of Pakistan's shifted support to the United States and the United Kingdom. http://www.outpost-of-freedom. com/wtc00a.htm.

[85] November 3, 2001. UBL complains about the United States and the United Nations and warns that US/UN attacks divide the world. http://news.bbc.co.uk/2/low/ world/monitoring/media_reports/1636782.stm. Additional BBC commentary is bolded. This piece aired on Al Jazeera Network on November 3, 2001.

[86] Henry Bayman, *The Secret of Islam* (North Atlantic Books, 2003) liii.

[87] Abdullah Yusuf Ali, *The Holy Qur'an: Text, Translation, and Commentary* (Amana Corp., 1991) 103.

[88] Abdullah Yusuf Ali, *The Holy Qur'an: Text, Translation, and Commentary* (Amana Corp., 1991) 103.

[89] *Los Angeles Times*, Saudi Arabia: Bin-Laden, Others Sign Fatwa to Kill Americans" Everywhere. 23 Feb, 1998.

[90] Wakin, Malham. *War, Morality and the Military Profession* (Westview Press, 1979) 242-258.

[91] Telford Taylor, *Nuremberg and Vietnam: An American Tragedy* (New York Times Book Co., 1970) Ch 3.

[92] ibid

[93] ibid

[94] ibid

[95] Wakin, Malham. *War, Morality and the Military Profession* (Westview Press, 1979) 242-258.

[96] M. Wakin, War, *Morality and The Military profession* (Westview Press, 1979) 247.

[97] ibid

[98] ibid

[99] ibid

[100] ibid

[101] ibid

[102] Kellog-Brand Act, 1928.

[103] *History of the United Nations War Crimes Commission*, (London, HMSO) 1948.

[104] Joseph McKenna, *Ethics and War: A Catholic View (Random House, 1960) 214.*

[105] *National Public Radio interview with Reverend J. Bryan Hehir on Jan 25 2002 on the subject of "A Just War".*

[106] Gary Wills, *What is a Just War?* (Yale University Press2004) 27.

[107] *National Review Online: Justice in War Just-war Theory*, Kathryn Jean Lopez, October 15, 2001.

[108] ibid

[109] ibid

[110] ibid

[111] *National Public Radio interview with Reverend J. Bryan Hehir* on Jan 25 2002 on the subject of "A Just War".

[112] Gary Wills, *What is a Just War?* (Yale University Press, 2004) 41.

[113] Quoted in Elshtain, *Just War Against Terror*, 131.

[114] Samuel P. Huntington, *The Clash of Civilizations and the Remaking of World Order* (New York: Simon and Schuster, 1996) 256. (also quoted in *The Virtue of War*)

[115] *International Law on Bombing Civilians*, (www.dannen.com/decision/int-law.html) Nov 16, 1999.

[116] Kenneth R. Timmerman, *Preachers of Hate* (Three Rivers Press, 2004) 5.

[117] RAND, *U.S. Countermeasures Against International Terrorism*, March 1990.41.

[118] Michael A. Ledeen, The War Against the Terror Masters (Truman Talley Books, 2003) 147.

[119] Benjamin Netanyahu, *Fighting Terrorism* (Farrar, Straus and Garous, 2001) 132-148.

9-12-21

Printed in the United States
117505LV00004B/184-270/P